UNIVERSITY OF NORTH CAROLINA
STUDIES IN COMPARATIVE LITERATURE

THE CHALLENGE OF COMPARATIVE LITERATURE

NUMBER 51

BY THE SAME AUTHOR:

Spiritualismus und Sensualismus in der englischen Barocklyrik. Braumüller, Wien, 1932.
Werden und Wachsen der U.S.A. in 300 Jahren. Politische und literarische Charakterköpfe von Virginia Dare bis Franklin D. Roosevelt. Francke, Bern, 1939.
Dante's Fame Abroad, 1350-1850. The Influence of Dante Alighieri on the Poets and Scholars of Spain, France, England, Germany, Switzerland and the United States. Storia e letteratura, Rome, 1950; University of North Carolina Press, 1950 and 1960.
Australia in Western Imaginative Prose Writings, 1600-1960. University of North Carolina Press, 1967.

IN COLLABORATION

History of German Literature, by Werner P. Friederich, with the Collaboration of Oskar Seidlin and Philip A. Shelley. Barnes and Noble, New York, 1948; Second Edition, 13th Printing, 1970.
Bibliography of Comparative Literature, by Fernand Baldensperger and Werner P. Friederich, 1950. Reprinted by Russell and Russell, New York, 1960.
Outline of Comparative Literature from Dante Alighieri to Eugene O'Neill, by Werner P. Friederich and David H. Malone. University of North Carolina Press, 1954; Fourth Printing, 1967.

TEXTBOOKS

Die Schweiz. Lippincott, Philadelphia, 1938.
Kurze Geschichte des deutschen Volkes. Crofts. New York, 1938.
The American Short Story. Francke, Bern, 1940.

EDITOR

Yearbook of Comparative and General Literature, vols. I - IX, 1952–1960. Reprinted by Russell and Russell, New York, 1966.
Comparative Literature: Proceedings of the Second Congress of the International Comparative Literature Association, Chapel Hill, 1958, 2 vols. Reprinted by Johnson Reprint Corporation, New York, 1970.

THE CHALLENGE OF
COMPARATIVE LITERATURE

AND OTHER ADDRESSES

by

WERNER P. FRIEDERICH

Edited by William J. DeSua

Introduction by David H. Malone

CHAPEL HILL
THE UNIVERSITY OF NORTH CAROLINA PRESS
1970

If justification beyond that of their intrinsic merit is needed for gathering together the addresses in this volume, it rests in the fact that their author has been involved in no small way in shaping the course and nature of the comparative study of literature in the United States since the second World War. Part I of this book presents, in effect, some of the major documents of the history of comparative literature by one of its chief participants, while Part II collects some of his examples of its practice. Together they illustrate (to paraphrase what T. S. Eliot said of Dante's contribution to the Italian language) that Werner Friederich is not only a master of his discipline but its servant as well.

Even those of us who may not entirely subscribe to his convictions in their every detail can appreciate the value of precisely those same convictions in establishing comparative literature as an autonomous discipline in our academies in days when its very *raison d'être* was imperiled by parochial interests. Those of us who know Werner Friederich personally—and the *Tabula Gratulatoria* bears witness to their ranks and cosmopolitan range—are thus doubly privileged in that we are celebrating both the success, qualified though it may be, of a cause in which he played a leading role and at once the sixty-fifth birthday, on June 2, 1970, of a distinguished colleague who is also a cherished friend.

Composed and delivered as they were over a span of years, the addresses in this volume inevitably contain some repetitions that could not be altogether eliminated without damage to the author's original conception. Blame for their inclusion, however, should be charged only to the editor's lack of surgical wit. My gratitude for permission to publish several essays in their entirety is extended to the *Journal of English and Germanic Philology* for "Late Renaissance, Baroque or Counter-

Reformation", to the *Jadavpur Journal of Comparative Literature* for "The Political Failure of the German Late Romanticists," and to *AUMLA* for "The Changing Attitude of American Authors towards Europe." Some of the remaining essays are revised versions or combinations of articles originally published in journals acknowledged in the appropriate chapter footnotes. I must also thank the University of North Carolina Research Council for its generous support of this publication.

My special and deepest gratitude goes to David Malone for his warmly elegant introduction, and to Mrs. Iris Friederich for her collaboration in selecting and emending these addresses while entering into a wifely conspiracy of silence against her husband about their publication. Without their invaluable help, this small tribute to a large achievement would not have been possible.

WILLIAM DESUA

The University of North Carolina at Chapel Hill

TABLE OF CONTENTS

This book is not just a collection of essays. It is also a significant part of the history of Comparative Literature since World War II. The amazing growth in Comparative Literature during the past quarter of a century has resulted from a variety of causes, including such things as the increased speed and ease of world transportation, changing political attitudes, new educational objectives, and so on. But the initial stimulus to that growth and much of the continuing momentum have derived in large measure from the dedication, energy, and leadership of the author of the essays contained in this book: Werner Paul Friederich, Kenan Professor and former Chairman of Comparative Literature in the University of North Carolina.

In both the literal and symbolic sense Werner Friederich's literary interests and philosophy grew out of the main tradition of Comparative Literature in Europe. He was, as it were, born a comparatist. Receiving his early education in his native Switzerland, he came to regard literature as the product of broad cultural traditions that encompassed far more than the history of a single nation. At the Sorbonne, and more particularly in his later contacts with Fernand Baldensperger and Paul van Tieghem, the cosmopolitanism of his native upbringing was subjected to the discipline of the methodology of Comparative Literature which had been developed in France. But neither the multilingual background of his Swiss education nor the methodological rigor of France can explain the almost evangelistic fervor with which Mr. Friederich undertook the advocacy of Comparative Literature in the United States.

That fervor seems to have been the product on the one hand of Mr. Friederich's Americanization and on the other of his profound, innate commitment to the universality of human values. He came to the

United States during the period of American Isolationism. A few years after finishing his Ph. D. at Harvard in 1932, he went to teach at the oldest state university in the U.S.A. in the small southern town of Chapel Hill, where the students were indeed isolated, and not just politically. Before he could do much about fighting either Isolationism or more especially the isolatedness of literary study in American universities, Mr. Friederich felt he had to learn more about the American traditions to which he would join his European ones. One of his earliest books was *Werden und Wachsen der U.S.A. in 300 Jahren*,[1] an introduction to American cultural history for German-speaking people in Europe. Writing this book was a kind of renewed initiation into the American experience which reinforced Mr. Friederich's own idealism and his dedication to human dignity.

World War II brought to an end America's political and economic Isolationism, but academic isolatedness in the teaching of literature remained a firmly established part of American education. Comparative Literature, whose development had seemed so promising early in the century, had become all but non-existent in the United States. Professor Arthur Christy of Columbia University worked for the revival of Comparative Literature through the establishment of a Comparative Literature Committee within the National Council of Teachers of English and by means of a *Comparative Literature Newsletter* which he edited from 1942 to 1946. But Professor Christy's death in 1946 seemed to signal the final collapse of Comparative Literature in the United States.

It was precisely at this moment that Werner Friederich's humanistic dedication, broad literary perspective and background, and phenomenal energy made of him 'ein rettender Engel,' as Ulrich Weisstein called him.[2] In 1945 Mr. Friederich had published a plea and a program in the *AAUP Bulletin* under the title "The Case of Comparative Literature."[3] With the death of Professor Christy, Mr. Friederich assumed the leader-

[1] Bern, 1939.
[2] *Einführung in die Vergleichende Literaturwissenschaft* (Stuttgart, 1968), p. 60.
[3] Vol. XXXI (1945), 208-219.

ship in carrying out the program he had himself proposed. He began with an informal newsletter of his own, mimeographed and mailed at his own expense, addressed to anyone who wished to identify himself as interested in Comparative Literature. The varied and enthusiastic response to this newsletter justified and reinforced his fervor. At the peak of this organizational activity, Mr. Friederich had some 350 regular correspondents. On the basis of this widespread interest Werner Friederich led Comparative Literature within a single decade from virtual oblivion to the beginnings of its present prominence in American higher education.

Through the support stimulated by his newsletter, he was able in 1947 to convince the Executive Council of the Modern Language Association that it should establish a Comparative Literature Section. The Comparative Literature Section, under his leadership, then sought a co-sponsor for an American scholarly journal, which it found in the University of Oregon, where *Comparative Literature* began appearing in 1949 under the editorship of Chandler Beall, with Werner Friederich as co-founder and Associate Editor. Even as he was engaged in all of this exhausting and exhaustive professional activity, he was working on another part of his program: the preparation of the first bibliography of the field since the second edition of the Betz-Baldensperger *Essai bibliographique* of 1904. Mr. Friederich had taken over the bibliographical notes, with about 15,000 items, which Baldensperger had been collecting for decades, but which he had never prepared for publication. The resulting Baldensperger-Friederich *Bibliography of Comparative Literature* (Chapel Hill, 1950), with some 33,000 entries, owes far more to Werner Friederich, and to his first wife Molly, than it does to Fernand Baldensperger.

The MLA Section, the journal, and the bibliography all represented considerable progress, but not enough. In 1952 the informal newsletter became *The Yearbook of Comparative and General Literature*, founded and edited through its first nine years by Werner Friederich. The *Yearbook* provided the means by which American scholars interested in Comparative Literature could explore what their discipline was: its definition, its purposes, its limitations, its methodologies. Through all of the theorizing and arguing that took place in the *Yearbook* Mr. Friederich remained faithful to his catholic breadth of perspective and his respect for the dignity of others. While most were joining the "French" camp or the "American" camp, or various outposts of either, Mr. Friederich could write, "The horizons are thus wide enough to enclose within the scope of our field a multitude of scholars with similar cosmopolitan ideals, but with a wide variety of plans and methods to translate these ideals into tangible reality."[4] He had from the first sought to reconcile differences and to convince apparently opposing camps of scholars that their common interest in literature was of far greater significance than their differences over methodology. From the late Forties he had been working, not just with American scholars, but with European scholars as well, always finding the common ground of interest beneath the superficial tangle of differences.

Mr. Friederich's work with European scholars led to the organization of the International Comparative Literature Association, which held its first Congress in Venice in 1955. It was the Second Congress of the International Comparative Literature Association, held in Chapel Hill in 1958, that marked the culminating success of Mr. Friederich's dedicated activity, and this Congress itself was planned, organized, and managed by him. Ten years later, in his Presidential address to the American Comparative Literature Association meeting in Bloomington, Harry Levin identified the Chapel Hill Congress as "an occasion which may be said to have dramatized America's coming-of-age in comparative literature."[5] Since the Chapel Hill Congress Comparative Literature has indeed flourished in the United States beyond anyone's expectations. Today we tend to take for granted the steady increase in student enrollments in Comparative Literature, the steady increase in books about Comparative Literature, even the gradual growth in bureaucratic strength of Comparative Literature in American colleges and universities. We take even more for granted the years of work and

---

[4] "Our Common Purpose," *infra.*, p. 23.
[5] "Comparing the Literature," *Yearbook of Comparative and General Literature,* No. 17 (1968), p. 12.

struggle which made the successes of the last decade possible. If today we look back to the beginnings we can fully understand what André M. Rousseau meant when, in 1963, he wrote in a review of the Stallknecht-Frenz *Comparative Literature, Method and Perspective*: "Le temps paraît déjà loin où W. P. Friederich était accueilli à Paris en 1948 comme le Christophe Colomb du comparatisme américain. Bibliography, Year-book, Société Nationale, congrès de Chapel Hill, sont maintenant com-plétés par le premier manuel destiné aux étudiants . . . ."[6]

Having devoted so much of his own time and energy to the develop-ment of Comparative Literature, Mr. Friederich was ready to leave the field of professional battle as soon as victory was certain. He served as President of both the International Comparative Literature Association and of the American Comparative Literature Association and then withdrew somewhat from the professional scene, confident that the success for which he had prepared the way would grow steadily under fresh leadership.

Werner Friederich's evangelistic advocacy of Comparative Literature sought to break down the artificial linguistic and political barriers that had so confined the study of literature in the first half of this century. But throughout his career he has fought against any such barriers that would confine his own study of literature. Even while he was involved in the late Forties in so much organizational work and in the monumental task of compiling *The Bibliography of Comparative Literature*, he was himself studying Spanish and Italian literature, in addition to his teaching of German and Comparative Literature at the University of North Carolina. He spent a year doing research in Seville and Florence, and in the same year that saw the *Bibliography* published, he completed his *Dante's Fame Abroad, 1350-1850* (Rome, 1950). Fulbright Professorships in Australia in 1955 and 1964 were the occasion for his becoming widely read in Australian literature, which he has since repeatedly tried to get the northern hemisphere to recognize. But only those of us who have been lucky enough to study with Werner Friederich can know the unlimited

[6] Review of Newton P. Stallknecht and Horst Frenz, *Comparative Literature, Method and Perspective* (Carbondale, Illinois: 1961) in *Revue de Littérature Comparée*, XXXVII (1963), 111.

range of his cultural interests or his total dedication to the human values which the study of literature should support. Indeed, some of the energy which has gone into his advocacy of Comparative Literature derives from his conviction that, not just literature, but humanity itself should be freed from artificial confinements.

Something of Mr. Friederich's dedication, wide-ranging interest, and humanity can be found in this collection of essays. The essays do not so much embody the history of Comparative Literature since World War II as constitute a kind of running gloss on that history. The first six essays provide Mr. Friederich's developing ideas about the nature and purpose of literary study. It is no accident that the earliest two essays should be concerned largely with problems of professional organization and reviews of what was going on in the profession, and that the last essay of Part One should be concerned with the "Humanizing Influence of Literature." All of Werner Friederich's energy and effort have been dedicated ultimately to making it possible for literature to enrich, enliven, and humanize more and more individual lives.

In contrast to the essentially programmatic and methodological articles of Part One, the essays of Part Two deal with a variety of comparative literary problems mostly from the viewpoint of *Geistesgeschichte*. These articles were originally prepared as public lectures given at universities around the world, from Sevilla (1950) to Berkeley (1962), and from Singapore (1955) and Calcutta (1959) to Vienna (1960) and Perth and Kyoto (1964). Like the essays in Part One, those in Part Two reflect some of the author's fundamental professional purposes. All of Mr. Friederich's scholarly writing has sought to synthesize human knowledge, to provide a greater understanding of the part in relation to the whole, to show the universality of literary values, and to reveal the essential unity of the human experience throughout history and throughout all of literature. Again it is no accident that the first lecture in Part Two should discuss the literature of Mr. Friederich's native Switzerland and that the last should look back on Europe through the eyes of American authors. Steadily as one moves through the essays in Part Two the perspective seems to expand, until one can see all literary expression as a manifestation of mankind as a whole, speaking necessarily in different tongues and different modes and idioms of expression, but giving voice to what is common to all men.

Those who joined Mr. Friederich's crusade for Comparative Literature almost twenty-five years ago, the thousands of students who studied with him at Chapel Hill—or while he was a visiting professor at Bern, Hawaii, Zürich, Berkeley, Colorado, Duke, and Southern California— and his many colleagues and friends around the world will welcome this collection of lectures. Some of these friends are listed in the *Tabula Gratulatoria* in this volume. This book will help all of us to realize the truly remarkable progress which Comparative Literature has made since World War II; it will remind us of the warmth, understanding, breadth of learning, and compassion which we came to know in the author himself; and it will strengthen our confidence that Werner Friederich's vision will be fulfilled that the literature of all men belongs to all men and can become a principal means for their realizing their common humanity.

DAVID H. MALONE
University of Southern California

TABULA GRATULATORIA

Helen Adolf
Pennsylvania State U.

Danilo Aguzzi-Barbaglio
Tulane U.

Antonio Alatorre
El Colegio de México

A. Owen Aldridge
U. of Illinois

D. C. Allen
The Johns Hopkins U.

Walter W. Arndt
Dartmouth C.

José Arrom
Yale U.

J. A. Asher
U. of Auckland, N.Z.

S. C. Aston
FILLM, St. Catharine's, Cambridge

Stuart Atkins
U. of California, Santa Barbara

Anna Balakian
New York U.

Ivan Barko
Monash U., Victoria

Yvonne Batard
U. de Rennes

Albert C. Baugh
U. of Pennsylvania

Marcel Bataillon
Collège de France

Max I. Baym
Brooklyn Polytechnic Institute

Chandler B. Beall
U. of Oregon

Naseem A. Beg
UNESCO, Paris

Lienhard Bergel
Queens C., Flushing

Angelo P. Bertocci
U. of Iowa

Konrad F. Bieber
State U. of New York, Stony Brook

Louis E. Bittrich
Texas Lutheran C.

Haskell M. Block
Brooklyn C.

Leslie Bodi
Monash U., Victoria

E. Boecker
American U. of Beirut

D. H. Borchardt
La Trobe U., Victoria

Buddhadeva Bose
Calcutta

Claude Bouygues
U. of British Columbia

xvi

xviii

Saburo Ota
Tokyo

George P. Parks
Queens C., Flushing

Charles Passage
Brooklyn C.

Carlo Pellegrini
U. di Firenze

Henry Pettit
U. of Colorado

Rupert Pickens
U. of Kentucky

Burton Pike
Cornell U.

George Pistorius
Williams C.

Henry Pochmann
U. of Wisconsin, Madison

Giuditta Podestà
Genova

Jacinto do Prado Coelho
U. of Lisbon

Robert A. Pratt
U. of Pennsylvania

Lawrence M. Price
U. of California, Berkeley

W. W. Pusey
Washington and Lee U.

Olga Ragusa
Columbia U.

Warren Ramsey
U. of California, Berkeley

Dale B. J. Randall
Duke U.

Daniel Reedy
U. of Kentucky

Arnold G. Reichenberger
U. of Pennsylvania

Herbert W. Reichert
U. of North Carolina

Henry H. H. Remak
Indiana U.

Bodo L. O. Richter
State U. of New York, Buffalo

Erwin R. Ritter
U. of Wisconsin, Milwaukee

Jacques Roos
U. de Strasbourg

Ralph Rosenberg
Yeshiva U.

C. Dana Rouillard
U. of Toronto

André Rousseau
U. d'Aix-Marseille

Jean Rousset
U. de Genève

Horst Rüdiger
U. Bonn

Frank G. Ryder
Indiana U.

Herman Salinger
Duke U.

Midhat Šamić
U. of Sarajevo

Richard and Helen Samuel
U. of Melbourne

Vittorio Santoli
U. di Firenze

Aldo Scaglione
U. of North Carolina

Derek P. Scales
Australian National U.

Margaret Schlauch
U. of Warsaw

W. A. G. Scott
Monash U., Victoria

Oskar Seidlin
Ohio State U.

Karl-Ludwig Selig
Columbia U.

Alfred Senn
U. of Pennsylvania

Robert Shackleton
Bodley's Librarian, Oxford

Philip Allison Shelley
Pennsylvania State U.

Sam M. Shiver
Emory U.

Ernest J. Simmons
Columbia U.

J. Carlyle Sitterson
Chancellor, U. of North Carolina

Jacob Smit
U. of Melbourne

W. A. P. Smit
U. of Utrecht

Ian H. Smith
U. of Tasmania

James M. Smith
Emory U.

Sidney Rufus Smith
U. of North Carolina

Jean J. Smoot
U. of North Carolina, Raleigh

E. L. Stahl
The Queen's C., Oxford

Ria Stambaugh
U. of North Carolina

Rudolf Stamm
U. Basel

Lionel Stevenson
Duke U.

George Winchester Stone, Jr.
New York U.

Heinrich Straumann
U. Zürich

Albrecht B. Strauss
U. of North Carolina

F. W. Strothmann
Stanford U.

Gleb Struve
U. of California, Berkeley

Maria Strzałko
U. of Cracow

Ronald T. Sussex
U. of Canterbury, Christchurch, N.Z.

Petrus Tax
U. of North Carolina

Ransom T. Taylor
U. of Nebraska

Ruth Z. Temple
City U. of New York

Walter Thys
U. Ghent

Eugene F. Timpe
Pennsylvania State U.

J. H. Tisch
U. of Tasmania

Guillermo de Torre
Buenos Aires

Gerard Tougas
U. of British Columbia

Louis A. Triebel
U. of Tasmania

PART ONE

I. COMPARATIVE LITERATURE IN THE UNITED STATES[1]

I am very glad and grateful to be given a chance to tell this distinguished *Congrès international d'histoire littéraire moderne* about the recent American endeavors in the field of Comparative Literature and, in particular, to extend to all of you our cordial invitation to collaborate with us in our effort to make the first visible result of our recent labors, our new journal *Comparative Literature*, a fine scholarly publication. But before speaking of this particular purpose of my coming to Paris, allow me to give you a brief outline of our doings during the past few years which have so happily resulted in a closer collaboration of all American comparatists and in the founding of our own periodical.

In the fall of 1945, mainly as a consequence of a programmatic article,[2] there began a movement which strove to unite, within the framework of the Modern Language Association of America, all scholars interested in an international and comparative approach to the problems of literature. The MLA, to be sure, for years had featured seven Discussion Groups devoted to Comparative Literature (Prose, Popular Literature, Arthurian Literature, The Renaissance, Anglo-Franco-American, Anglo-German and Franco-German Literary Relations), but these seven Groups acted without cohesion and lacked a firmly organized Comparative Literature Section to unite them, to derive strength from the hundreds of professors participating in these

[1]Paper read at the *Quatrième Congrès d'Histoire Littéraire Moderne*, Paris 1948, and printed in the *Actes*, Paris, 1950.
[2]"The Case of Comparative Literature," *Bulletin of the American Association of University Professors*, 1945. See also my other articles on "L'organisation des 'comparatistes' aux Etats-Unis," *Revue de Littérature comparée*, XXII, 1948, 115-21, and "Zur Vergleichenden Literaturgeschichte in den Vereinigten Staaten" in *Forschungsprobleme der vergleichenden Literaturgeschichte*, ed. by K. Wais and F. Ernst, Niemeyer, Tübingen, 1958, 179-91.

3

seven isolated Group Meetings and, in turn, to give new strength and purpose to the cosmopolitan ideals animating these men and women. At the MLA meeting in Chicago in December, 1945, therefore, some thirty enthusiasts decided to select a small group of respected scholars who would sponsor our petition to be admitted as a new and integral part of the MLA and whose very prestige would help us in bringing together, in the new Comparative Literature Section, all scholars of good will who were anxious to break down the barriers between the various language and literature departments in American colleges and universities and to emphasize instead the many literary traditions which unite rather than separate us. These sponsors of our movement, carefully chosen in order to present as wide a cross-section as possible of our country and of the academic departments involved, were the following: Messrs. D. C. Allen (Johns Hopkins, Neo-Latin literature), A. B. Benson (Yale, Scandinavian literatures), J. Carrière (Virginia, French literature), C. Gohdes (Duke, American literature), R. S. Loomis (Columbia, Medieval literature), L. M. Price (California, German literature), E. J. Simmons (Columbia, Slavic literatures), J. R. Spell (Texas, Spanish literature), D.T. Starnes (Texas, English literature), Stith Thompson (Indiana, Folklore), B. L. Ullman (North Carolina, Greek and Latin literatures), G.C. Wood (Dartmouth, Italian literature), and A. E. Zucker (Maryland, Oriental influences).

During the past three years, the membership in our unofficial organization increased steadily and encouragingly, and the mimeographed Newsletters sent out at regular intervals finally reached a roster of more than 350 colleagues. These Newsletters, serving as the sole bond during our formative years, discussed many moot points: the difference between Comparative Literature and General Literature; the insufficiency of our own offerings in the various universities and, above all, the lack of interest shown both by university administrators and members of the various literature departments; the question of whether or not to encourage so-called courses on "World Literature" on a distinctly undergraduate level; the desirability of founding our own journal to give expression to our ideals, etc. Many of these matters were discussed at a second gathering of comparatists during the MLA

4

meeting in Washington in December, 1946. The increasing unity of our opinions and plans seemed to augur so well for the future that I was elected as the first chairman of the Comparative Literature "Section" with the request to continue the publication of my Newsletters until success had been achieved.[3] And in March, 1947, the Executive Council of the MLA informed us that our new Section had been acknowledged and accorded a definite place in the annual programs of the Association. Thus we had completed the first stage of our program within twenty months of its inception.

Various factors contributed to support our efforts to secure a more widely acknowledged place for Comparative Literature at home and abroad. For instance, right from the beginning we enjoyed the active support of many of our colleagues in Canada—men like Messrs. Viatte (Laval, Quebec), Noad (McGill, Montreal), Denomy, Joliat and Rouillard (Toronto), Kirkconnell (McMaster, Hamilton), and Clark (British Columbia, Vancouver), whose interest and encouragement were deeply appreciated. I may add that in the United States, French scholars, heirs to a great tradition in Comparative Literature,—men like Messrs. Guérard (Stanford), Chinard (Princeton) and Peyre (Yale) —likewise came to our help when we needed their counsel and assistance.

It should also be noted that American interest in "World Literature" was stimulated as early as 1940 by the late Professor A. E. Christy of the University of Illinois, who worked with the National Council of Teachers of English (NCTE) in an effort to familiarize his colleagues with the relations of foreign literatures to the Anglo-American cultural bloc and to acquaint them, too, with the best English translations of foreign masterpieces. Professors of English literature constituted the bulk of Professor Christy's organization, and in the *Comparative Literature Newsletters* published by this group (which, unfortunately, were discontinued some time after Mr. Christy's death) pedagogical and scholarly articles were equally represented. Though there are great

[3]Professor Stith Thompson was chairman in 1948 and in 1949, and Professor R. Wellek in 1950.

differences of principle between this branch of the National Council of Teachers of English and our own Comparative Literature Section in the MLA, I should like to hope that in the years to come we will derive mutual profit from a certain amount of collaboration between the two.

Many annual bibliographies published by leading American journals constitute another important factor which helped prepare the ground for the gratifying success of our own labors. Most of the bibliographies of a distincly comparative character are compiled by members of our new Section. Among the most important I should like to mention: the Americana Germanica published in the *American-German Review* (A. E. Zucker, Maryland), the Franco-German Bibliography in the *Bulletin of Bibliography* (R. Rosenberg, Yeshiva), the Anglo-French and Franco-American Bibliography in the *French-American Review* (D. Bond, Chicago), the Bibliography of Italian Studies in America, published in *Italica* (V. Luciani, New York), the Anglo-German Literary Bibliography in the *Journal of English and Germanic Philology* (L. M. Price, California), the Bibliography of Critical Arthurian Literature in the *Modern Language Quarterly* (J. Parry, Illinois), the American Bibliography and Research in Progress in the Modern Languages and Literatures, published in the *Publications of the Modern Language Association of America*, the Folklore Bibliography in the *Southern Folklore Quarterly* (R. Boggs, North Carolina), and the Renaissance Bibliography in *Studies in Philology* (H. Craig, North Carolina).

With the founding of the Comparative Literature Section and its official acknowledgement by the Executive Council of the MLA, the seven Comparative Literature Discussion Groups have at last found a common bond to promote their interests—and the professors at American universities and colleges who are members of different academic departments and also of various other Sections and Groups within the MLA have at last found an organization which allows them to mingle freely with their English, French, German, Spanish, or Slavic colleagues, and to discuss with them questions of significance to all. In order to make quite sure that the new Section would always serve as a clearinghouse and safeguard the interests of all constituent members, it was

6

decided that the annually elected chairmen of these seven Groups should always, *ex officio*, serve as the Advisory and Nominating Committee of the new Section—for only such a plan as this assures us of the greatest and smoothest coordination possible.

Two other great problems had to be faced after the successful conclusion of the first phase of our activity: the founding of a Comparative Literature journal of our own, and the finding of ways and means to increase the somewhat battered prestige of Comparative Literature in America. We suffer from the great disadvantage that independent Departments of Comparative Literature are practically unknown in American institutions of higher learning. Most of our members belong to English, French, or German departments, in charge of courses on distinctly national literature, and they busy themselves with certain comparative problems or courses only insofar as time and inclination permit. Being left entirely to themselves, without encouragement by the administration or by their immediate colleagues, many professors in the 1920's, unmindful of the clear distinction between Comparative Literature and General Literature, decided to foster nothing but introductory courses in English translation, and the preponderance of such courses (Dante, Cervantes, Racine, or Goethe in English translation, or "The Drama from Aeschylus to Ibsen") contributed greatly to the general decline of the prestige of "comparative" studies in America, which seemed to waive foreign language requirements and did not really investigate a poet or an epoch from an international point of view.

To be sure, during the past few years very encouraging developments have taken place in many individual universities, which allow us to hope that our ideals, espoused by leading institutions and supported by our new national organization, may gradually spread all over America and initiate the growth of a sound internationalism in the field of literary scholarship. Yale University, for instance, recently established a Department of Comparative Literature under the chairmanship of Professor R. Wellek; and Harvard finally reorganized its Department of Comparative Literature (which had been inactive since the departure of Professor Baldensperger) and among the men assisting Professor

7

H. Levin, its chairman, are scholars like Messrs. Poggioli, Bush, Viëtor, Munn, Seznec, (to mention only the members of our new Section). In the Middlewest, the Department of Comparative Literature at the University of Wisconsin is being reinvigorated under the chairmanship of Professor G. Orsini, and at Indiana University a new department will begin to function under Professor H. Frenz.

Indiana, incidentally, combines sound scholarship on the graduate level with the system of offering vast introductory courses on World Literature to hundreds of its undergraduates. This fast-spreading post-war development of offering more and more lectures on World Literature will be well worth watching, because it is clear that such elementary courses will, in turn, stimulate our advanced work in Comparative Literature proper, for it stands to reason that in the long run only well trained Ph. D. 's in Comparative Literature (and not hastily recruited members from the English Departments) will be able to conduct these courses soundly and satisfactorily. In the South, our University of North Carolina may well serve as a sample of the somewhat unsatisfactory arrangement often encountered with regard to Comparative Literature: it possesses an active department of Comparative Literature (which is more than most American Universities have) whose courses are clearly divided between General Literature (for undergraduates) and Comparative Literature (mainly for M. A. and Ph. D. candidates), but it has no budget of its own and its ten or twelve professors are merely lend-leased from other departments, owing their primary allegiance and responsibility to those departments rather than to Comparative Literature proper. At Carolina, too, as well as all over America, much remains to be done to bring about sounder departmental conditions, and—to shift our attention from administrative to academic considerations—much remains to be done, too, to convince our colleagues in the Humanities that Comparative Literature no longer simply means easy introductory courses in English translation, that its hard scholarly principles and requirements in fact are more exacting than those of any other department, and that a flourishing Department of Comparative Literature, more often than not, will give them valuable help in their own investigations of national literatures. And yet we can face the future with

8

confidence, for Americans, like the Swiss and the Dutch, are basically ideal comparatists. Away from the national rivalries of strife-torn Europe, they have no special axe to grind and can weigh the debits and the credits of the various national literatures justly and with detachment. Furthermore, with the blood of most European nations flowing through their veins, they have a possibility of achieving a tolerance and a level-headedness in their outlook which at times is missing among militant European scholars.

All these hopes will take years to reach full fruition. In the meantime, it is most encouraging to report that the third phase of our program —the founding of a Comparative Literature journal of our own—met with an early and promising success. We had in the beginning appointed a journal committee to investigate the financial and academic problems involved in the launching of such an undertaking and, backed up by a national organization that knew what it wanted to achieve, we were able to take advantage of a generous offer from the University of Oregon and to make plans to start publication in January, 1949. The full title of the journal is as follows: "*Comparative Literature*—A Quarterly Journal published by the University of Oregon, with the Cooperation of the Comparative Literature Section of the Modern Language Association of America." Professor Chandler B. Beall of the University of Oregon and I are serving permanently as Editor and Associate Editor, respectively; the five members of the present Editorial Board are Messrs. H. Hatzfeld (Catholic University), V. Lange (Princeton), H. Levin (Harvard), A. Warren (Michigan), and R. Wellek (Yale). I can describe the aims of the new journal no better than by quoting a few sentences from its first announcement: "Founded at a time when the strengthening of good international relations is of paramount importance, *Comparative Literature* provides a forum for those scholars and critics who are engaged in the study of literature from an international point of view. Its editors define comparative literature in the broadest possible manner, and accept articles dealing with the manifold interrelations of literatures, with the theory of literature, and with broad views of movements, genres, periods, and authors—from the earliest times to the present."

In particular—and in conclusion—I should like to say that my colleagues in America want me to emphasize to you, with all the sincerity and persuasive power at my command, that we are very anxious to collaborate with you and to be of help to you wherever and whenever we can. Of course, allow me to assure you that we do not wish to interfere with, or to compete with, the splendid work the *Revue de Littérature comparée* has been doing here in Europe. All we want to say is this: that to a post-war Europe sorely beset by financial difficulties and by an extreme dearth of paper and of scholarly journals, we shall be glad to extend our helping hand and to incorporate in our journal a reasonable number of articles written not by North American but by European and South American scholars, and that to this end we are willing to accept contributions not only in English, but also in French, in German, in Italian, and in Spanish.[4] For somehow we feel, with joy and with pride, that what we are doing is part of the deeper meaning of the Marshall Plan, that our vigorous activity somehow goes beyond the realm of mere book-learning, that we are here to help each other, to understand each other, and to save, together with you, the great cultural heritage that belongs to us, the Western World.

[4]Of the forty-four articles published in *Comparative Literature* during the first two years of its existence (1949-50), thirty are in English, eight in French, three in Spanish, two in German, and one in Italian. Articles from the following European scholars have been published by us: five from England (by Professors Lytton Sells, Entwistle, Chicoteau, Willoughby and Wilson), three from France (by Professors Vermeil, Babelon and Tosi), three from Italy (by Professors Rebora, Praz and Toffanin), two from Spain (by Professors Cioranescu and Alonso Cortés), one from Germany (by Professor Curtius), one from Switzerland (by Professor Strich) and one from Hungary (by Professor Hankiss).

II. THE FIRST TEN YEARS OF OUR COMPARATIVE LITERATURE SECTION IN THE MLA[1]

The friends, sponsors, and organizers of our Comparative Literature Section met here in Washington exactly ten years ago. It can do no harm to sketch briefly just how much ground we have covered in the past decade, for that will allow us all the better to see what still remains to be done in the next ten years.

A first small gathering at the MLA meeting in Chicago in 1945 had not produced more than a handful of comparatists; but a good crowd with definite proposals attended at the Washington meeting in 1946, and in the Detroit meeting of 1947 we were for the first time given a tentative place on the MLA program. It has been a long and rather arduous uphill fight, fought mostly by means of some forty different mimeographed letters which, in the course of these years, I sent to about 350 selected members of the MLA. It is one of the ironies and the tragedies of Comparative Literature that it seems to flourish only after the catastrophes of World Wars, when men are sufficiently aroused to denounce the folly of political or cultural chauvinism and to advocate a far more tolerant program of literary internationalism instead. French comparatists achieved and consolidated their strength in the wake of the First World War and of the League of Nations; it was obvious for us in America that we had to strike while the iron was hot and while men, after 1945, had not yet sunk back into the lethargy of indifference and that kind of political provincialism and of academic departmentalization which we all resent as wrong and self-defeating.

[1]Address delivered at the meeting of the Modern Language Association of America in Washington in December, 1956, and reprinted from the *Yearbook of Comparative and General Literature VI*, edited by W. P. Friederich and Horst Frenz, Chapel Hill, 1957, 56-60.

In the New York meeting of 1948 we became an integral part of the MLA—and it is our foremost task to stay that way, strong and progressive. In order to consolidate our efforts within the framework of the MLA in particular and of American academic life in general, we decided, after mature consideration, that the Advisory Committee of the Comparative Literature Section should *always* consist of the seven chairmen of the seven already existing Comparative Literature Discussion Groups, for that would give us an enviable compactness and unity of purpose in building up our field and in facing any unfavorable new trends that might develop. This is the only complaint I will have to make in this short address: that this cautious system was *not* preserved, and that a few years ago the Advisory Committee was constituted from among former chairmen of this Section. That means that the seven Comparative Literature Discussion Groups have been cut off, that they are left to manage alone, as best they can; that we, the Section, are not here, as we should be, to hold them together and to give them a common goal. In the interest of greater unity and therefore greater strength I would urge the chair to restore the former system, to keep faith with the sponsors and the organizers of ten years ago, so as to be able to face the years ahead with a better coordination and unanimity of purpose.

A second goal remained after the Section had been established, the seven Groups coordinated, and a strong bond had been formed among all MLA members who believe in an international approach to the study of literature: journals had to be founded in which we could give expression to our ideals and which would serve as a further link between all of us. Two publications have appeared in the last few years to take care of this. First, through the financial generosity of the University of Oregon we were able to constitute an Editorial Board and to plan the publication of *Comparative Literature*, a quarterly journal which publishes "articles dealing with the manifold interrelations of literatures, with the theory of literature, and with broad views of movements, genres, periods, and authors." A somewhat more prosaic yet equally useful task is assigned to the *Yearbook of Comparative and General Literature*, published by the University of North Carolina Press since 1952, which supplies the reader with an annual bibliography of Comparative

Literature, with articles discussing the scope and the methods of Comparative Literature, and with presentations of the various Comparative Literature departments and curricula in American universities and colleges.[2] Both the journal in Oregon and the *Yearbook* at North Carolina, incidentally, are sponsored by our Comparative Literature Section here in the MLA—and the *Yearbook* is also sponsored by the Comparative Literature Committee of the National Council of Teachers of English, a body of friends and colleagues whose collaboration we may be able to secure ever more firmly as the years go by. It should also be noted that the annual Bibliography contained in the *Yearbook* is increasingly taken care of by the various group-bibliographers of our Comparative Literature Discussion Groups.

The third big step was, of course, the forging of close ties with our fellow-comparatists abroad—with the flourishing Comparative Literature setups at the French and Dutch universities and with the strong Comparative Literature Society of Japan. Largely as the result of French efforts there was established in 1954 the International Comparative Literature Association (ICLA), with headquarters in Paris; it held its First International Congress in Venice in September, 1955. Since our Comparative Literature Section here does not possess a budget of its own, outside the MLA, we could not join the International Association in Paris as a body, but those of us who believe in it and want to support it can do so individually, at a membership rate of $1.50 per year. Until now the ICLA has enrolled about 80 members in America and about 100 in Europe—and membership in that international organization also entitles each American participant to the Oregon journal and the North Carolina *Yearbook* at a reduced rate.

The big and very happy news in connection with the International Association is, of course, that the Second International Comparative Literature Congress will take place here in America, at the University of North Carolina in Chapel Hill around September 8, 1958. The

[2]After its ninth issue (1960), the *Yearbook* was transferred to Indiana University, where it continues to be published under the editorship of Horst Frenz. Russell and Russell, Inc. in New York is in charge of re-issuing the out-of-print Chapel Hill and Bloomington numbers.

13

Ford Foundation and to some extent also the American Council of Learned Societies have given us two very generous grants in order to make the Congress really international, *i.e.*, to enable us to pay the transatlantic passage of almost fifty foreign comparatists, mostly Western European, with a few delegates from Japan, South America, and Eastern Europe. The University of North Carolina plans to make this five- or seven-day meeting as attractive as possible, with a planned sightseeing trip from New York and Washington to Jefferson's Monticello and along the Skyline Drive to the Smoky Mountains National Park and the Cherokee Indian Reservation. That, and your wholehearted cooperation, should make this meeting memorable and extremely worthwhile for foreigners as well as for us, and it will at any rate be the first time that we in America will be able to play host to a large body of overseas delegates and give them an insight into American hospitality and the values of American university life. All further inquiries about the ICLA and its Congress September 8-12, 1958, should be addressed to me; a mere postal card will result in your receiving all the necessary information.

These, then, are some of our main achievements during the past ten years: national organization, professional publications, international contacts. One thing becomes amply and perhaps painfully clear as we look at this record: we have certainly done enough, more than enough, in organizational matters. I know that many of us have often been criticized for apparently caring far more for the outer shell than for the real kernel—the scholarly productivity which alone can make Comparative Literature great, beautiful, and inspiring. Yet we all should remember that first things must come first, that we desperately needed this national and international frame and organization in order to give to all of us and to our field stature and standing in our own institutions. We had a few great comparatists in the 1920's and the 1930's—yet what, really, did they achieve? They were like voices in the wilderness; they had nobody to back them up, no journals to uphold their scholarly ideals, no friends at home and abroad. We at least, in the 1950's and 60's, will not suffer from that deadly disadvantage—and if we fail, if any one of us fails on his own campus, it will be because of his own or his own immediate superiors' personal shortcomings, and not because there was no respected organization to lend prestige, encouragement and support to his efforts.

As opposed to the three goals of the first decade, I should like to propose—among several possibilities—just one goal for the second decade ahead of us, in order, through singleness of purpose, to emphasize all the more its very vital importance for our future development: the long overdue improvement of the concept and of the teaching of Comparative Literature in every single American institution where Comparative or General or World Literature is taught. The very fact that there exists such a choice of words to indicate a vaguely international approach to literature certainly means that our search for accurate definitions must continue and that we must separate the wheat from the chaff. It cannot be my task here to go into these problems beyond saying that we must raise our standards, harden our requirements, and reconsider our values.

It may not be necessary to worry about the curricula for an M. A. and a Ph. D. in Comparative Literature; let us assume for a moment that the half-dozen American universities giving graduate degrees in our field know what they are doing and that all is well. But we certainly do have to worry about what is being done on the undergraduate level in the name of Comparative Literature, for, more often than not, the goals are far too ambitious, the means inadequate, the results deplorable. If, like his colleagues from the Classics or the Romance departments, the comparatist is drafted to lend a hand in the teaching of the increasingly fashionable so-called World Literature courses, he should acquiesce and agree with those who suggest that he is perhaps best qualified to teach this kind of survey, while emphasizing at the same time that this, of course, is not his real job, that World Literature is *not* Comparative Literature and that, at best, these undergraduates are merely getting a superficial introduction into the hard and challenging field of real comparative work that may follow later. A comparatist, I think, should be even more jealous of his soundness and good reputation than most other university people—and this honesty should induce him, if part of his work must consist of survey courses, to rename these courses, calling them Great Books courses rather than using that extravagant term, "World" Literature. When he is teaching them, his integrity should again induce him to choose a few reprints of entire texts, and not feel satisfied with multitudinous little excerpts from anthologies. And, turning from his purely introductory work for sophomores and juniors to his real work as a comparatist, he will also realize that for seniors and graduate students he must severely limit his scope and dig well below the surface. With few exceptions, he will wish to restrict courses in English translation to lower classmen or to certain upper classmen minoring in Comparative Literature, and he will try to inculcate in his seniors as well as in his graduate students a sense of solidity and achievement by analyzing a small number of subjects, problems, movements, or genres that are common to various literatures—in the original language whenever humanly possible.

If he does that, if he measures his success by depth rather than by vague generalizations, then we need not fear for the future of Comparative Literature in our universities and colleges. Of the two criteria which will determine the fate of Comparative Literature in the years ahead, I can give advice only on one: sound, solid teaching. The other, sound solid research and publications, will take care of itself: a man's publishers, readers, and critics will tell whether he is good or not. But with regard to his teaching, he might feel encouraged if he knew that our organization is anxious to back him up in his quest of ever higher standards. Ultimately, when full success is achieved, I should like to visualize a system whereby a few comparatists will be assigned to every institution of higher learning—men who complement the efforts of their colleagues, the professors of English, German, Russian or Italian, by taking care of the one particular field of the literary relations between these languages and nations. Every Humanities Division should have on hand a few specialists devoted to the task of showing what the various literatures taught at a college or university have in common, what they gave to, and borrowed from, one another and how, each in its own way, they are spiritual heirs to, and important representatives of, our Western tradition.

As to the large majority among us who are not primarily comparatists, but primarily professors of English, Romance, or Germanic literature—they will surely agree with what we all know to be true, with an observation which may perhaps be trite, but which this entire assembly may well wish to repeat over and over again to all chairmen, deans, and presidents: namely, that their secondary interest in Comparative Literature, in their classwork as well as in their research, does not constitute an act of disloyalty to whatever literature department they are supposed to be working for. On the contrary, their occasional branching out into the relationships with neighboring literatures actually makes them better men and wiser scholars. A comparatist, by the very nature of his work, should be a distinguished asset amidst his overspecialized colleagues in French, English, and German departments. That is not only true, but a constant challenge to us, to work so as to keep it true.

III. OUR COMMON PURPOSE[1]

Recent discussions on the essence of Comparative Literature in this *Yearbook* have done much to clarify many moot questions and, if read in conjunction with European viewpoints expressed in recent issues of the *Revue de Littérature Comparée* and the *Germanisch-Romanische Monatschrift*, they indicate the road we have travelled since the days of Posnett's first (and now quite untenable) definition of the term Comparative Literature. On the other hand, however, these discussions have also pointed to serious cleavages among us which should not be permitted to develop too far, for the literary—and, I might add, the political—ideals which hold our heterogeneous group together are far stronger and more lasting than occasional divergencies concerning the goals and the methods of Comparative Literature.

Our teaching and, in part, our research in Comparative Literature vary widely, for they are largely circumscribed by the institutions in which we are located and by the type of students available on every campus. The courses given by us range from the lowliest sophomore class about the epic elements in the *Iliad* to the highest seminar for doctoral candidates about the aesthetic of European Symbolism. In our spare time, in our research, in papers read before our colleagues, in articles and books published for a wider audience, we reflect our own tastes, predilections and potentialities: some of us turn to thematology, others to an international study of genres; some prefer the investigation of influences, others turn to the importance of intermediaries; some try to link up their knowledge of two or three literatures with history or religion, others with the fine arts or with art criticism; some conceive

[1]Reprinted from the *Yearbook of Comparative and General Literature IV*, 1955, 55-59.

of the task before them as a useful excursion into the sociology of literature, while others are capable of permeating their work with the finest aesthetic considerations. It stands to reason that these differences of viewpoints produce works of differing quality and importance, for here again the articles and books may range from treatments of trifling themes to vast, comprehensive studies of great international movements; indeed, they may range from the pedantic to the obtuse. But each work represents what its author can do best, the kind of problem which he wants to choose in this fascinating, new, inviting field which is Comparative Literature. Already Muralt stated that "une des beautés de l'univers c'est la diversité" —and we can do no less than wish more power to each one of our colleagues, though his predilection may not exactly be our predilection. Though we in America are today increasingly agreed in rejecting the almost scientific rather than aesthetic approach of our deserving French forerunners in Comparative Literature, it surely will serve no good purpose if, in lieu of their views, we establish a rigid American canon of our own do's and don'ts. Our methods, within certain limits, are and should remain as free as our scholarly integrity permits.

In spite of the obvious variety of our interests, we are all resolved to break away from narrow departmentalization, that bane of colleges and universities, that breeder of national conceit and ignorance, and we are united in recognizing our fellow men across national borders, in acknowledging the very real significance of their culture and literature, and in studying the impact they have had on us and we on them. I am sure that all of you recall, as I do, classes in Chaucer which consisted of picking out Kentish or Northumbrian dialectal forms in the text and in which words like Ovid, Italy, France, the Renaissance were never even mentioned—or classes on New England Transcendentalism which were given in a complete vacuum, with no reference to German Idealism or European Romanticism. Today an increasing number of us are determined to put an end to such blindness, to place a national movement into its larger international context, to shake off the self-complacency and ignorance foisted upon us by departmental barriers and to learn a handful of foreign languages, and learn them well, if thereby we obtain the tools of enlarging our knowledge of literature and of enriching our own life as well as the lives of our students. If, in possession of his newly acquired faculties, a comparatist wants to rush into the field of thematology, we might agree with others who hold that the study of the different treatments of the same theme is not really Comparative Literature at its best—though we cannot help observing, too, that, for instance, the presentation of the ever advancing evolution of the concept of the rights and the dignity of womanhood in the treatments of Jephthah's daughter or of Griseldis is most rewarding, and that any student of Vondel or of Dekker could profit by studying some later versions. Or if another comparatist chooses to derive rather sweeping generalizations about national tastes and literary predilections from the investigation of the success or the failure of a great dramatist like Racine or Shakespeare, or of a literary movement like Classicism or Romanticism in various nations, we should consider this also to be entirely legitimate and desirable. Equally acceptable are occasional political interpretations of the popularity or the unpopularity of a certain nation in the literatures of its neighbors. Such efforts to connect literature with the multiple political or social activity of the world around us would certainly obviate the reproach, frequently heard, that the Humanities in general and Literature in particular have ceased to attract the youth of today because they operate in a vacuum, an ivory tower removed from all reality—and the comparatist, who is doubly qualified to approach these questions on a broad international front, can be expected to produce more fascinating and more accurate results than most of his colleagues.

Of course, it is agreed that the proper study of literature is literature, and that the investigation of the traffic of ideas and forms across national boundaries will never absolve the comparatist from the necessity of studying the texts themselves, of fathoming the genius and the intellectual and aesthetic greatness that are behind every great work of art. My own rather strong convictions in this matter are that we should always go back *ad fontes* and that we should never neglect the aesthetic evaluation of a poet—but that we should not overdo it, either. The study of Comparative Literature, of the manifold cosmopolitan interrelationships of literary trends, is enough of a task for any one man; to go beyond that is certainly the exception, not the rule. In our age of specialization, we comparatists have a definite task assigned to us which we should fill to the best of our abilities; in our teaching, in the vast majority of all cases, if we are good campus-diplomats, we cannot and dare not encroach upon other territories. In the importance of our field, we are on an equal footing with our colleagues in the Italian, German and French departments; we should help each other, complement each other, but, if possible, not poach in each other's territory. Our colleagues in Italian, German or French supply us with all the biographical information, the textual criticism, and the poetic evaluation of a Dante, Goethe, or Hugo, while in our classes we supply the international background of the Renaissance or of Romanticism, the crisscross of currents between Italy, Germany and France that helped to make Dante, Goethe and Hugo what they are. I believe that most of us are satisfied with that kind of task; in most cases we would be glad if the individual literature departments acknowledged the dire need for such complementary work and urged us to take care of that particular mode of investigation for which our training has prepared us.

To go beyond this limited assignment and to say that the term "Professor of Comparative Literature" (apart from the old objections to the term "comparative") is really a misnomer and that "Professor of Literature" would far more accurately define our calling is something with which, I imagine, only few people would agree. Most of us are not big enough to assume this super-role of evaluating literature in its well nigh boundless totality—and even if we were, we might suddenly find out that it would not be good diplomacy to wish to assume it. We should be content if the individual universities acknowledge us as being on an equal footing with the professors of Greek, Spanish or American literature—but we most certainly do not wish to supersede them, to appropriate their jobs in addition to ours, and to push them out of their vested interests. That would be suicide, for it would utterly destroy the goodwill and the friendly collaboration so many of us have been trying to build up during the past decades—and before we knew it, we might be back where we started from a generation ago: in the wilderness. The Schlegels with their all-encompassing universality would have qualified as "Professors of Literature," and in our times that title might possibly be bestowed upon certain practitioners of the art, like Archibald MacLeish or T. S. Eliot—but when it comes to scholars, we would do better keep to our special training and assignment.

A few examples will show how the professor of national literature and the comparatist can complement each other, each one practising his own special skill while at the same time learning and borrowing from the other: Mr. Chamard's excellent life of du Bellay and Mr. Vianey's study on Italian Petrarchism in France; Mr. Kittredge's or Mr. Craig's work on the basic greatness of Shakespeare and Mr. Par's investigation of Shakespeare in Spain; Mr. Strich's analysis of German Classicism and Romanticism and Mr. Baldensperger's tracing of the movement of ideas during the French Revolution. It does not matter who came first among the two types of scholars, the "nationalist" or the "internationalist," for such beneficial influences occur in either direction. This is the type of co-existence we should strive to achieve; these are the fields in which we can be peers among peers.

There is another reason why we should be satisfied with our task and not impinge—to choose an example at random—upon the New Critics in their cult of evaluating the imagism of Ezra Pound's poems or the symbolism of Kafka's novels: our own age, with the old tragedies and the new hopes of its post-war adjustments, is in dire need of constant reassurance of the political and cultural unity of our Western World. It would seem that today we can afford less than ever to indulge in many fads of subjective aestheticism, for what the younger generation needs is a constant awareness of the cultural unity of all Western civilization and of the constant and fructifying give-and-take that occurs between the great literatures of our world. We may no longer be as boldly optimistic as Wendell Willkie was with his "One World!" concept, but at least we are firmly determined to consolidate the spiritual unity in our half of the world—and in that task Comparative Literature can be of immense importance. Indeed, it may be assumed that many of us have deserted the study and the teaching of individual national literatures not only because we found the narrowness of cultural and academic departmentalization often frustrating, but also because we have espoused a political ideal and because, within the limits of our profession, we want to do our share in the realization of the cherished goal of Western unity. This may be a slightly utilitarian perversion of our primary task, of which, however, we need not be ashamed. In justifying this semi-political aspect of our chosen calling, we realize that it would again be unnecessarily dogmatic—and not in keeping with the tolerant latitude which we are willing to accord to all of our colleagues—if we frowned upon those comparatists who prefer other emphases to the West European-American relations which are dearest to most of us; for those who work in Oriental-Western or indeed in Slavic-Western relations form an equally important element in our present task of breaking down barriers and of building bridges.

The horizons are thus wide enough to enclose within the scope of our field a multitude of scholars with similar cosmopolitan ideals, but with a wide variety of plans and methods to translate these ideals into visible reality. If the comparatist has any "enemies" whom he should combat with all his night, it is not the hapless colleague who loves thematology, or delves into comparative national psychologies, or traces fussy little influences through fussy little intermediaries. Far more dangerous to our cause is the professor of Spanish who teaches his literature as though nothing important had ever happened north of the Pyrenees, or the professor of English who, partly because of his own linguistic inabilities, does not deign to look at what has been thought and written across the English channel. If we can win over these men to a belated emulation of our program, we may be able to reform also the few "enemies" within our ranks who are not a credit to our earnest purpose. Foremost among those I would mention, on the undergraduate level, the teachers of survey courses who pretend to give grandiose courses taught by means of anthologies, with scanty sprinklings of infinitesimal fragments ranging from the *Gilgamesh* epic to just one chapter of *War and Peace* or one act of *The Doll's House*. And on the graduate level our main concern should be with professors who, when given a chance to do comparative work, do so in order to satisfy some dormant jingoism and to carry into literature old political hatreds and prejudices—something which we should consider with profound distaste as the very negation of our finest purpose.

But such matters can be settled by earnest discussions on individual campuses or at national meetings. They need not for one moment disrupt what should be most important to all of us: the basic unity of all comparatists, of all believers in the international approach to literature.

IV. GREAT BOOKS VERSUS "WORLD LITERATURE"[1]

I am sure that all of you present here will join me in extending our sincere gratitude to the University of Wisconsin for having made possible our getting together under the aegis of the National Council of Teachers of English and discussing the very challenging problem of teaching so-called World Literature courses in English translation.

For that task, that goal of teaching the great masters of World Literature, is by no means easy to achieve. Your group is constantly being doubted and heckled on two fronts: on the left by nationalists and isolationists who cloak their own intellectual inability ever to look beyond the frontiers of their own chosen literature in the mantle of patriotic ardor—for, far worse than the relatively tolerant Thoreau, "they travel much—in Concord" and therefore see no reason why they should bother with the literature of the world at large. And on the other hand, there are the most high-minded comparatists among us who attack your group because they insist that World Literature in English translation is *not* Comparative Literature and that it must always be restricted to undergraduate instruction (and I agree with these two assertions)—and therefore they look down upon World Literature courses and perhaps deny their legitimacy (and with this attitude I do *not* agree.) At this meeting, I am sure, we all will quite lustily attack the nationalists in the Humanities, for to be narrow-minded is the very negation of the concept of Humanism, and so they deserve to be over-

[1]Largely reprinted under the title of "On the Integrity of Our Planning" from *The Teaching of World Literature, Proceedings of the Conference at the University of Wisconsin*, April 1959, edited by Haskell M. Block. Chapel Hill, N. C., 1960 and Johnson Reprint Corporation, New York, 1966.

whelmed with criticism from all sides. But, after this attack on the left flank, there should be an opening towards the right, a never-tiring attempt to establish a *modus vivendi*, a constructive and profitable relationship between World Literature courses and Comparative Literature.

In fact, I should like to emphasize at once that I tried to build a bridge between Comparative Literature and World Literature some eight years ago when I founded the *Yearbook of Comparative and General Literature* which began to appear in Chapel Hill in 1952. That *Yearbook* was born out of a certain sense of disappointment, because our journal, *Comparative Literature*, in Oregon decided to remain true-blue comparative. I was voted down, six to one, when I suggested to our Editorial Board that we should attempt an opening to the left and collaborate with certain colleagues who, to be sure, might not be "comparatists" in the strictest sense of that word, but who shared with us an enthusiastically cosmopolitan approach to literature. When this suggestion was turned down, I got in touch with my friend Horst Frenz from Indiana and other internationalists in the NCTE—and the *Yearbook* was started simply because it seemed imperative that you and we should learn to understand each other and to work together. Horst Frenz, the loyal Associate Editor, suggested that it should be called *Yearbook of Comparative and World Literature*—but since, as you will soon notice, I do not particularly like the term World Literature and since, at any rate, it would not have been judicious to wave, shall we say, a red flag in front of those very men whom I hoped to lead to the altar with you, we finally settled on the term *Yearbook of Comparative and General Literature*. The only trouble is that I do not quite know what General Literature is, and for years I have been trying to find a learned article by some learned man who would unscramble the various definitions by Van Tieghem, Wellek, Guérard and others of what General Literature really encompasses, so that, in retrospect, we will at last know what exactly our *Yearbook* is supposed to do. In the meantime, in spite of the absence of a proper definition, we publish in Part I of every *Yearbook* articles on the scope and the methodology either of Comparative Literature or of World Literature courses; in Part II we honor great representatives of the two groups—for instance, in your case, men like Philo Buck or Arthur Christy; in Part III we give descriptions of departmental planning and "états présents des travaux" both of Comparative and of World Literature curricula in at least twenty American universities; in Part IV, exclusively for your group, we provide useful reviews and evaluations of the most recent English translations of world classics; while Part V, mostly for the comparatists, contains an annual supplement to the basic Baldensperger-Friederich *Bibliography of Comparative Literature* of 1950.

But to return to our topic, namely the enemies on your left and on your right. Let us not, upon second thought, attack the enemies on your left, for they are discredited enough: the Anglicists whose world stops at the cliffs of Dover, the Hispanists or Italianists who would never look beyond the Pyrenees and the Alps respectively; the Germanists and the "Francisants" for whom the Rhine used to be a ditch deeper than the Grand Canyon. They and their American counterparts are definitely on the way out—in New England and even in the Old South perhaps more so than in the Middle West. Let us, instead, dwell on the two groups closest to our hearts: the Comparative and the World Literature people, and let us, at this very meeting, attempt again to draw them closer together. Which, in the last analysis, perhaps means, to put it bluntly, that *my* friends should surrender some of their pride and begin to practice the Christian virtues of understanding and cooperation —while ever so many among *your* friends should acquire greater respectability and integrity in their academic endeavors. For surely, that which unites us, our faith in a common great cultural heritage of mankind, which we should gratefully acknowledge and share with our peers in distant lands, and our utter abhorrence of what Professor Guérard has so aptly called literary McCarthyism, is far stronger than what divides us. In fact, if we reduce our problems to the simplest formula, there should be absolutely nothing to separate us from the moment we recognize clearly that World Literature courses in English translation in 99% of all cases should be undergraduate courses, and that out of this preparatory labor there then may—but not necessarily will—grow distinctly comparative courses for our graduate students. From the moment we recognize this, all our arguments should be over—for surely people of our kind should not, in the back-alleys of our own American institutions of higher learning, indulge in petty fights about irrelevant qualitative distinctions between ourselves. A few years ago, I preached a little sermon on that in an article entitled "Our Common Purpose" contained in the 1955 *Yearbook*—and I do not need to repeat myself.

With the bond of friendship and mutual respect thus firmly established between our two groups, I hope that it will not be amiss to discuss what I should call sound and useful courses in English translation. For we are faced with such an abundance of possibilities here in America, that we may well envy the Europeans where—apart from far greater linguistic versatility—mere geographical facts may induce the Swiss to be concerned with such neighbors as Germany, France, and Italy, but not with Spanish literature, because there is no common border between the two—while the Spaniards in turn may disregard such geographically or ideologically distant lands and literatures as those of Russia or Poland. We, in America, on the contrary, are facing Europe as a whole, as the cradle of our civilization, as the former homeland of all our people—and thus Sweden and Portugal, Yugoslavia and Holland are no less important to many among us than the Big Two or Three of that continent. And, so, what should be chosen?

The foremost consideration surely is to choose the classical Greek and Latin literatures in English translation. It is bad enough that Greek and Latin keep on fighting a losing battle for decent survival; let us not add to this tragedy by disregarding the rich heritage of classical Antiquity that is available even in English translation. Whether teachers of World Literature or of Comparative Literature, we are and must remain the most loyal, the most respectful friends of our Classics Departments, giving them a never-tiring moral support against all the perversions of academic values that may emanate from our Education or Commerce departments. That, then, seems an absolute must; if nothing else, our curricula must offer the great Greeks and Romans in translation.

Little need be said about the customary great literatures of Europe which, in one form or another, should be offered in translation to all those non-language majors who have a love of literature and are entitled to know about it, even if they cannot read their texts in the original. Perhaps I might remark that only French literature is of a constantly sufficiently high quality to deserve a complete survey course from beginning to end—while with the other literatures we might go into depth rather than width. Germany, for instance, in spite of the Golden Age of Barbarossa and the deep significance of the Reformation, would offer the richest harvest in the 200 years from Lessing to the Weimar Republic. Even narrower, and therefore deeper, could be the basis for Italy, Spain, or Russia—let us say merely the *trecento* and the *cinquecento* for Italy, the *Siglo de Oro* for Spain, from Charles V to Philip IV—for surely if, instead of piling up endless lists of meaningless names, the student knows the Renaissance of the former and the Counter-Reformation of the latter, he has begun to grasp the very soul, the very quintessence of Italy and Spain. That is after all what he wants —for, remember, if he wants to know more than that and become a specialist, he has no business being in a translation course. As to the soul of Russia, we find it best in the novel of the nineteenth century —and that should be enough. Indeed, quite often the contribution of an entire nation might be built around the life and works of one single man—and thereby constitute yet another variety in depth rather than width of those courses: for Scandinavia, for instance, I am thinking of a very detailed study of Ibsen—which, in a way, would become an analysis not only of Norway, but of the whole technique of the modern drama in general.

Things get far more difficult when we come to Asian literatures—for how many among us are linguistically qualified to teach such courses? In spite of our desperate need to know far more about Asia than we actually do, we are in a particularly deplorable predicament at present —for the sons of Christian missionaries in China or India who grew up bilingual are slowly dying out, while the bright young men trained by our State Department have, for obvious reasons, not yet begun to forsake their political assignments and to turn to the teaching of Asian cultures and literatures instead. Nevertheless, if our universities are so bold or so farsighted as to want you to venture into the field of Asian cultures and literatures in translation, I would point to four distinct centers of which each one, separately, deserves at least one full semester course to begin with: the Muslim World, especially the Arabs, though one might extend this to Iran and perhaps even farther east; India, China and Japan. To devote less than one semester to any of these four centers would be unworthy of our academic standards.

From these remarks about great literatures in English translation, from Greece to France to Russia to India, I should like to derive various observations and discuss them in some detail.

First, even for undergraduate novices, do not use anthologies unless they deal exclusively with lyrical poems, and, above all, do not ever bandy around that awfully facile and arrogant concept of World Literature courses. For just as snippets from *Antigone* or *Strange Interlude*, the sixth book of the *Aeneid* or the twelfth chapter of *Crime and Punishment* will never teach anybody the real greatness of Sophocles, O'Neill, Virgil or Dostoevski, so the term World Literature will never fool student or teacher that anybody can ever get even an inkling of the world's literature. Latin America, Africa, Australasia are always immediately left out *in toto*; Asian countries like Japan and China are skipped in favor of a few passages from old Sanskrit texts of India; of what is left, namely the so-called Western World, entire blocs extending from Finland to Poland and Bulgaria are likewise omitted, and only what I sometimes mockingly call NATO-literature is included, from ancient Greece through the Mediterranean and German literatures to the modern Anglo-Americans. We are daily offending untold millions of Muslims, Hindus and Buddhists by defining supreme virtue with just one arrogantly exclusive term, namely "Christian"; the citizens of the United States are again constantly offending their Mexican or Peruvian neighbors by arrogating to themselves alone the term "Americans" — and we must not haughtily establish a World Literature Club, a field so earnestly taught and distorted, and then promptly exclude nine tenths of all national literatures. Small voices have a right to be heard, too, even though the limitations of our understanding may not make us wish to be bothered by them. When Goethe in January 1827 coined that unfortunate term of "Weltliteratur" — a concept only, not a detailed academic program—he must have thought of a purely abstract and very distant possibility, as he did when he discussed with Schiller his equally elusive pet-idea of an "Urpflanze". It is not for us, for we can see only a few facets, and never the totality of God's whole creation. Neither for its content, nor for its poetic beauty will such a list of mere samplings from various nations make a lasting impression upon our young students —and that means that we miss the whole purpose of a course. To be sure, they would acquire a flimsy knowledge—less than a nodding acquaintance—with maybe thirty or sixty of the world's great poets —but that, sometimes, can be worse than nothing. All the more so since our students probably likewise know next to nothing about the great political, national, or historical background of these authors and the twenty-five centuries covered—and thus our work is quite as bad as though it were written on sand or water.

Instead, in our age of cheap paper-back classics, it stands to reason that, if such big trans-national surveys of literature are really ordered by the Humanities Division and the Dean's Office, we should substitute Great Books courses instead. Let us give up the idea of total coverage and strict historical coherence; let us, instead, after a lot of soul-searching, devise a program of, say, twelve great masterpieces for an entire academic year, and let us give at least eight to ten hours to each of them. The fine choice of these masterpieces which, after further mature consideration, may be changed in different years, should perhaps emphasize the genre first and explain, by means of completely read paper-backs, the quintessence of epic, of tragedy, of comedy, of novel—or, perhaps, in the only anthology to be tolerated in that course, of lyrical poetry. Next, by its very selection, the course might turn to explaining the distinctly unique contributions of individual nations—the Greek tragedy, the Roman epic, the Spanish picaresque novel, the Italian comedy. Likewise, a discussion of at most twelve authors during an entire year would also permit one to say something about the greatness of true giants in literature—Aeschylus, Virgil, perhaps Chaucer, Molière, Schiller, Dostoevski. Finally there might be time to illustrate, again by means of these same twelve authors, the basic meaning of Antiquity, Middle Ages, Renaissance, Classicism, Romanticism, Realism, Naturalism. In such a way, a survey course could really serve a multitude of purposes; the student would learn to read entire masterpieces under guidance, he would learn to know about genres and literary movements, he would be initiated into the rudimentary beginnings of literary criticism – and he would surely be more informed instead of more bewildered when his initiation into literature is over. After that, if he is a non-language major, he could take a course or two of just one or two national literatures or authors in English translation – and, if he should be a language major, he would, of course, turn to his languages and to his literatures in the original. Either way, his Great Books course would have helped him enormously.

One more worried remark before we turn to far more pleasant and optimistic matters. Till now I have expressed my concern only with regard to courses, programs, and students – what we must do and must not do in order to preserve our professional integrity and the standards of our colleges and universities which should be getting higher as we face the rising influx of candidates, instead of constantly getting easier and more lax. But now we should also have a look at the men who will teach these courses. I am not fearful about the national literature courses in translation – those about French literature or the Russian Novel in the Nineteenth Century, or Homer in English, for I presume that these are always given by men from these departments and that all is well with these specialists. But what about The Great Books courses, or worse, the Surveys of World Literature from A to Z? Who is the A. W. Schlegel or the Paul van Tieghem among us to teach these? And worse: since these big survey courses are mostly on the sophomore level, with hundreds of students split up into scores of sections: who on earth are the graduate assistants and the youngish Ph. D.'s and quickly drafted assistant professors who can talk intelligently about the *Odyssey* epic in September, St. Augustine's *City of God* in November, Machiavelli's *Prince* in January, Voltaire in March, and Kafka in May? I do not even dare to answer this question – but I feel I must raise it, for we must ever be mindful of the enemies to the left and the enemies to the right who will denigrate whenever they can, and gleefully seize upon any weakness in your armor. And I submit, for your prayerful consideration, that the greatest danger to our personal and academic integrity—if we are really resolved to introduce these sweeping courses and to have them taught by one man alone instead of a committee of at least ten specialists —lies not only in actually forcing such courses into our curricula, but in not being able to staff them decently. Here again I beg you, if such courses must be, at least not to make them Surveys of World Literature, but more humbly and correctly to call them Great Books courses—for a young instructor, after a few years, might actually learn to master twelve or fifteen milestones in World Literature well enough to speak enthusiastically and inspiringly about them and their beauties. The cheap modern paper-backs make this procedure advisable; yet even there, I would advise the choice of only semi-great works from Aristophanes to Flaubert, for real giants like *The Divine Comedy* or *Faust* are best left to individual full-semester courses.

At our stage of knowledge, the World Literature people would do well to lower their sights and adjust themselves to other, more modest methods of the comparatists. This, for instance, they can also do by studying Comparative Literature in national or regional blocs. Thus, one specialist can take the relations between the Latin and the Germanic blocs as his province; another can go into inter-Slavic relations between the literatures of Russia, Poland, Yugoslavia or Czechoslovakia, or indeed into the fascinating area of what the West since Diderot and Herder has given to Russia, and what Russia since Pushkin or Turgueniev has given to the West. American comparatists can go into the regional problem of European-American relations, or, better still, into inter-American relations, *e.g.* the North American appreciation of the Nicaraguan poet Rubén Darío, or of the great Brazilian prose epic about desperate poverty, fanatic messianism and rebellion in *Os Sertões* or *The Backlands* by Euclides da Cunha, or the equally gripping Argentinian prose epic about Gaucho tyranny and invasions, namely Sarmiento's *Facundo Quiroga*, available in English translations under the title of *Life in the Argentine Republic in the Days of the Tyrants, or Civilization and Barbarism*. It is not for us to say what type of regional comparatism our Japanese colleagues should pursue; but instead of re-studying, over and over again, the impact of Western literatures since the opening of Japan in 1854, or the importance of men like Lafcadio Hearn, they might find it profitable to turn to earlier Japanese-Chinese relations, using Korean literature as a valuable intermediary. My friend Grove Day of the University of Hawaii, a frequent guest in Australia, has entered into a new form of regionalism which is legitimate and in many ways comparative, for he studies the Literature of the Pacific, in which many nations participate. At the University of North Carolina we have recently opened up a new field of which I am quite proud, and which I think is unique in America, for our Semitist, a native of Spain (mindful of the fact that he can never equal the rich Semitic departments of the type of the University of California at Los Angeles under von Gruenebaum) is collaborating with some of our hispanists in specializing just in the wealth of the three cultures and literatures that existed in medieval Spain—of Muslims like Averroes, of Jews like Maimonides, of Christian Spaniards like the Archpriest of Hita, author of *El Libro de Buen Amor*, or like Juan Manuel, author of the equally Orient-inspired *Conde Lucanor*.[2] This regionalism, in this case the Arabic-Catholic-Jewish heritage of medieval Spain, is about all a group of dedicated professors and students can fathom; everything else the World Literature advocates so glibly want us to do, would indeed expose us to the often heard and justified reproach that many so-called comparatists are superficial and unsound. We must have none of that.

These, then, in brief, are some of the viewpoints worth considering: that Foreign Literature in English Translation is a much needed field for undergraduate instruction, while Comparative Literature should be distinctly for graduate students only. Indeed, at North Carolina, we increasingly encourage comparatism only for graduates who already have a good knowledge of foreign languages and literatures, though we still do have a small number of undergraduates majoring in our field, too. Foreign Literature in English Translation might start with a Great Books course on the sophomore level which would initiate the

---

[2]This exceedingly promising program unfortunately had to be discontinued after a few years because of the multiplicity of philological courses required in the Department of Romance Languages.

average student into a few great authors, genres and national contributions; afterwards, as an upper classman, he should delve into narrower, yet deeper courses on the Orient or Greece, on the Spanish Golden Century or on Goethe. Whatever his later career may be, whether he will become a business man, a physician, or a professor of English—this will give him a truly liberal education. It will be a program of which we can all be proud. We internationalists in the teaching of literature, assembled here in this center of learning of the American Midwest, have a very important task indeed assigned to us: that of making American youth aware of the great literatures to the East and the West of us, of the throbbing and fascinating cultural interplay with the rest of the world, and of making our students approach the literary masterpieces of our friends with respect and with gratitude.

V. THE CHALLENGE OF COMPARATIVE LITERATURE[1]

Just as every well-run government has a department not only of Internal Affairs, to take care of its manifold internal problems and obligations, but also a department of Foreign Affairs for the constant scrutiny of its political and cultural relationships with the nations around it, so I think that every good University also should establish what is commonly called an inter-departmental Curriculum of Comparative Literature in order to remain perennially aware of the constant flow of ideas and literary works and influences across national and linguistic borders, and to redefine again and again the manifold credits and debits that occur in the field of literary cosmopolitanism.

What the individual literature departments are doing within the purview of their own aspirations does not concern us here. They may oscillate between two equally objectionable extremes, and either be totally pedestrian, enumerative, biographical and prosaic, or, as the New Critics would like them to be, totally subjective, detached, rhapsodic, caring naught about scholarly apparatuses and backgrounds, and stressing instead the unique personal impact upon their quivering selves of a work of art *in vacuo*. The sound solution, of course, between these two extremes, lies somewhere in the happy middle, endeavouring to combine the factual, cultural background which we acquired during our academic apprenticeship with an ever keen appreciation of, and attention to, the text, the work of art itself. The comparatist need not necessarily become involved in this kind of purely departmental fighting, though it should be clear that, because of his interest in influences

[1]Address at the Plenary Session of the Australasian Language and Literature Congress, Melbourne, August, 1964.

and international crosscurrents, it lies in the very nature of things that he would not be too fond of the New Critics.

Yet only with caution. If I may speak of a minor unpleasantness right here at the beginning, it is just this problem which has given rise to a certain argument between the French and the American comparatists. One need only look at the rich output of French comparatists since 1920, at the hundreds of articles in the *Revue de Littérature comparée* and the scores of monographs in the *Bibliothèque de la Revue de Littérature comparée* to perceive that the question of influences has always been uppermost in the eyes of the French comparatists. To Americans like René Wellek from Yale University, this ceaseless searching for sources and borrowings seemed far too dull, prosaic and mechanical, for it was apt to lose sight of the greatness and the uniqueness of a work of art *per se* and to get bogged down in an almost purely scientific classification of spiritual values which, as Aristophanes in his *Frogs* says of his comparison between Aeschylus and Euripides, cannot be weighed like mere pounds of cheese. It was to clarify the important problem of the scope and the methods of Comparative Literature and the different viewpoints held mainly by French and American scholars that, in 1952, in addition to the journal *Comparative Literature*, published in Oregon since 1949, I founded the *Yearbook of Comparative and General Literature* in North Carolina, in which definitions could be drawn up and compromises worked out, and I am happy to say that an important article on the two schools of Comparatism in *Yearbook IX* of 1960 by Henry Remak at Indiana University established at least a *modus vivendi* between French and American Comparatism. Yet let me repeat that this family quarrel occurs among internationalists on either side of the Atlantic, *i.e.* among men and women who believe in cosmopolitan cross-fertilization, and who smilingly agree with Paul Valéry's witty assertion that we all live and feed on others, and that even the lion is nothing but assimilated mutton — and that it does not occur with those extreme New Critics, who in their contemplation of a literary masterpiece, would disregard the fine variety of the chemistry of its creation. Such extremists would be apt to condemn Comparatism *a priori* as a violation of their creed.

This is not the time nor the place to speak of the origins of the comparative study of literature, except to say that it did not really get off the ground—*e.g.* with Dryden's *Essay on Dramatic Poesy*, or Voltaire's *Essai sur le poème épique*—as long as neo-classical prejudice held the authors in bondage. Only Pre-Romanticism and Romanticism provided an enthusiastic, universal and intuitive understanding of the poetry and the mentality of the most diverse nations and races which was free of false nationalism and condescension. Perhaps it was Switzerland which began this phase, with Bodmer's translation and defense of *Paradise Lost* and his pathbreaking essay *Ueber das dreyfache Gedicht Dantes*; with Mme de Staël's very significant *De l'Allemagne*, and further her pro-Italian outlook in *Corinne*, or with Sismondi's distinctly comparative *De la littérature du Midi de l'Europe*. Germany followed with Herder's great essay on Shakespeare, his folklore anthology *Die Stimmen der Völker in Liedern*, and his comparative study on *Homer und Ossian*; with A. W. Schlegel and his fine renderings of Shakespeare, Dante and Calderón and his increasing preoccupation with the literature of ancient India; with Goethe, who coined the dangerously challenging term of "Welt-literatur". Other nations continued the trend: *e.g.* de Sanctis in Italy, Longfellow in America, Georg Brandes in Denmark. Yet when all is said and done, it is to France that we owe our greatest debt, and it is in France, from Joseph Texte through Baldensperger, Hazard, van Tieghem, Carré, Bataillon and Roddier on, that Comparatism became a serious subject for academic study. The "Institut de Littérature comparée" at the Sorbonne has today only one younger brother in Europe, namely the "Institute for Comparative Literature" at Utrecht—while American Comparatism which, early in the century, began at Columbia, Harvard, Wisconsin and North Carolina and, after 1945, in scores of other institutions, has today probably reached its highest peak at Yale University.

I will not discuss the basically important booklet on what French Comparatism stands for, *La Littérature comparée* by the excellent scholar Paul van Tieghem; instead, I will concretely mention three works by Fernand Baldensperger in order to illustrate three basic modes of approach according to the French School. First, his *Goethe en France* indicates the enormous importance attached to the role of the emittor —the impact of Goethe's works from *Werther* to *Faust* on the whole

38

realm of French literature and mentality up to the twentieth century. Second, Baldensperger's *Les orientations étrangères chez Honoré de Balzac* dwells on the significance of the receiver in literature, by pointing to all the literary inspirations Balzac had received from the Latin, the Germanic, and the Slavic world. And third, of course, there is the valuable role filled by intermediaries, in this case by refugees, which Baldensperger traces in his very notable *Le mouvement des idées pendant la Révolution française*. It is this scientific, almost mechanical pinpointing of facts and credits and debits that has aroused Wellek's wrath — and Jean-Marie Carré, in a subsequent book called *Le mirage allemand dans la littérature française*, gave Americans further ammunition because it dwelt not so much on the literary, aesthetic and artistic aspects of the German impact in France, but on the bluntly sociological and political implications among French writers and journalists of pro-German propaganda from Mme. de Staël through Romain Rolland to the age of Laval. That, according to Wellek, is no longer Comparative Literature, not even literature. Hence the alarming title of his address at the Congress of the International Comparative Literature Association at the University of North Carolina in 1958, "The Crisis of Comparative Literature", in which he warns us against getting mixed up with all sorts of peripheral fields and thus losing sight of our main task: the artistic evaluation of a masterpiece. A simultaneous paper presented by a Japanese colleague who illustrated the influence of James Joyce in Japan (translations, imitations, articles and books about him, etc.) by means of statistical charts, as though the ups and downs of Joyce in Japan were comparable to a brokerage figure in Wall Street, only widened the cleavage between the largely Wellek-led American School and the Franco-Japanese School of Comparatism.

However, things are not quite so bad — and there are far more common convictions among comparatists, than there are differences of interpretation among them. A mere glance at the Baldensperger-Friederich *Bibliography of Comparative Literature*, a listing of more than 33,000 items, first published in 1950 and supplemented and enlarged in the North Carolina and Indiana *Yearbooks of Comparative Literature* ever since 1952, should convince any reader of the wealth and the real challenge of the comparative approach to the study of literature. To be sure, there are hundreds of pages devoted to emittors (*e.g.* Mr. Bataillon's *Erasme en Espagne*), receivers (the foreign sources of Boccaccio), or intermediaries —whether they be translators like Florio, travellers like Camoens, refugees like Mickiewicz, diplomats like Paul Claudel, or salons like those of Mme Necker or of Sophie d'Houdetot. But there is much more than that. There is the vast field of thematology, of "Stoffgeschichte" so greatly favored especially by the Germans: of Iphigenia, of Rome, of the Alps, of Joan of Arc, of Don Juan or of physicians, soldiers or nightingales in literature. There is the international investigation of literary genres and forms across centuries and linguistic barriers—of the sonnet, the historical novel, the apprenticeship novel, the bourgeois drama, the Virgilian epic, the satire in various literatures. There is, above all, the comparatists' attempt to grasp a great literary movement, if not in its totality, then at least in as many literatures as possible, as van Tieghem did with his admirable volumes on *Le Pré-Romantisme* and *Le Romantisme*—the question, for instance, of what distinguishes the Italian from the Spanish Renaissance, and those two again from the German Reformation; the question of whether there is an internationally coherent literature of the Baroque among those who are called Metaphysical Poets, "les précieux", Marinists, Góngorists —and, if so, what its common denominators are; the question of what distinguishes the Classicism of Racine from that of Goethe, the tempestuous Romanticism of ever so many Europeans from the almost ascetic New England Transcendentalism of the Bostonians; the problem of Realism in the various regional novels of "*Heimatliteraturen*" extending from Gotthelf in Switzerland and Verga in Italy to Bret Harte in California and Mikhail Sholokhov in communist Russia; the uncertainty whether Naturalism began not perhaps with Zola in France or Dostoevski in Russia, but 'way back with Rojas' *Celestina* in the Spain of Ferdinand and Isabella. And in the investigation of these international literary movements, let me hasten to add, it is often not at all important to dwell on influences that are actually demonstrable, but to find evidences of a so-called "*Zeitgeist*", of a spirit of the time which produced, independently of each other, similar mentalities and hence similar works and styles in the most diverse countries, whether it be Rococo or Impressionism.

Yet even a comparatist's concern with peripheral, not exclusively literary, matters does not bother me as much as it does some of my colleagues—for surely a student of literature who tries to grasp things horizontally, *e.g.* three to five literatures in a given century, rather than vertically, just one literature all the way from *Beowulf* to T. S. Eliot or from *Les serments de Strasbourg* to Proust, is in a better position than the professional monoglot to pass valid judgment on the tremendous impact of Darwinism, Marxism, or Freudianism upon the literature of the last 50 or 100 years. And to turn to other and perhaps even more acceptable peripheral fields of cultural history and their connection with *belles lettres* which the comparatist is especially well qualified to handle—there is Philosophy and its relationship with literature, *e.g.* the effect of Cartesianism upon the literature of the Enlightenment, the impact of Spinoza upon Romanticism, the importance of Schopenhauer or Nietzsche for our own age; there is History – either historians like Plutarch and his fructifying influence upon the entire Renaissance from Jacques Amyot and Montaigne to Lord North and Shakespeare, or great historical figures and events like the French Revolution and Napoleon, with their vast international reverberations extending from Foscolo and Goethe to Carlyle and Tolstoy's *War and Peace*; there are the Fine Arts—Painting, Architecture, Sculpture, Music—and the countless studies that can be made by scholars like Helmut Hatzfeld or Calvin Brown in America of their kinship to the literature of a given period —not to speak of Lessing's *Laokoon*, Ruskin, Pater or the Pre-Raphaelites. And last but not least, there is certainly the relationship between Literature and Religion, again a field in which the comparatist can open up far wider vistas than the one-literature-specialist, whether he deals with general religious epics like *La Divina Commedia* or *Der Messias* or, in particular, with the mystics from Thomas à Kempis to beyond Santa Teresa de Jesus, the Jesuit drama from le père Caussin to Avancini, the impact of the Bible upon Calderón or MacPherson, the Jansenism of Racine or Manzoni, the valiant religious battles of Pascal or Lessing, the Puritanism of Milton or Hawthorne, the aspects of atheism in Diderot or Shelley, the deism of Shaftesbury or Tom Paine, the role of quakerism in Voltaire or John Greenleaf Whittier, the despairing religious crises in Leopardi or Kafka—or, indeed, with the impact of the Inquisition or of the *Index librorum prohibitorum* upon Dante's *De Monarchia*, Machiavelli's *Principe*, Campanella's *Città del Sole* in Italy, *Lazarillo de Tormes* or the "erasmistas" in Spain, Luther or Fischart in Germany, Voltaire's *La Pucelle d'Orléans* or *Mahomet* in France.

In the enumeration of all these avenues of approach one feature may have struck you—as it did Mr. Baldensperger and myself when we compiled our *Bibliography*—namely that there are very few actual comparisons in the field called Comparative Literature. Simple comparisons *e.g.* between Vico and Herder or again between Balzac and Dickens—the similarities and dissimilarities between lives, characteristics, plots, ideas, styles—are possible, but not very inspiring, and they leave us with a vague So what? impression of dissatisfaction. Comparatists in general are apt to go cautiously on unrelated comparisons —just as, in the other extreme, they eschew tracing minute half-line metaphors from one poet back to another, or accumulating, for sheer cumbersomeness' sake, a score of *Cleopatra* tragedies or another score of *Miles gloriosus* comedies in the various literatures. They should and must look for more relevant connections between great authors, trends, and styles to make their work meaningful and valuable. The name "Comparative" Literature is therefore to a certain extent a misnomer, just as Baroque, Romanticism and Symbolism are sometimes called misnomers. They have been handed down to us and we are now stuck with them; but the main thing is that we know and define what they mean when we use them.

Let us turn now from the purely scholarly challenge of plunging into the vast international ramifications and reverberations of a great literary figure or genre or theme to the practical advantages of having a Curriculum of Comparative Literature in every university. You notice that I say Curriculum, and not necessarily Department, of Comparative Literature—for we are at our best as a group of well-trained comparatists rooted in various departments who, under the chairmanship of a dedicated, full-time comparatist[2] bent upon nothing but encouraging the international approach to literature, ask an affiliated classicist to prepare, if possible, a course on the influence of the Greek drama or of Ovid's works upon the post-Renaissance period; or a medievalist to prepare a course on the Arthurian cycle in England, France, Germany, down to Spain's *Amadis de Gaula*. Comparatists in modern literatures should be encouraged to give a course on the one period when their own primary literature was most enriching from an international point of view. For instance, an Italianist should deem it a privilege to be urged to speak of the enormous influence of the *trecento* and the *cinquecento* upon the Spain of the Marqués de Santillana to Garcilaso de la Vega, France from Laurent de Premierfait to Philippe Desportes, England from Chaucer to beyond Painter's *Palace of Pleasure* — an abundance of Italian literary influences that reached from Portugal to Hungary and Poland. A Hispanist can do the same for his two golden periods under the Arabs and again under Philip II and III, of which we find traces in Washington Irving's *Alhambra*, in Chateaubriand's *Le dernier des Abencerrages*, in Corneille's *Cid*, in Grimmelshausen's *Simplizissimus* or even in Butler's *Hudibras*. A "Francisant" can dwell on European literature just before and after 1700, when French Classicism and Enlightenment were the supreme inspiration for everybody, as far as the Russia of Trediakovsky and Sumarokov. The Germanist can stress the vast international significance of the Age of Goethe, from the Herder-disciples in Eastern Europe to the St. Louis Hegelians in America — and the Slavist with a knack for comparatism can dwell on what the West owes to the great Russian novelists, or vice versa. Even the often unwilling professors of English could learn to emulate all this (I should think that the richest period of English contributions to foreigners would be the eighteenth century); they can also go beyond, and study, for example, the deep English roots of American literature. Indeed, it would be comparatism of at least some kind if one studied the cross-

[2] We have grown at North Carolina since 1964, for at the present time our staff includes no less than six hyphenated comparatists (Professors W. J. DeSua, E. H. Falk, O. B. Hardison, A. Scaglione, R. Mayo) and eight affiliated professors.

currents and local peculiarities in the various literatures of the Common-wealth at large or, to turn to a different possibility, if one analyzed what new values the English-writing Irish from Goldsmith to Shaw and Joyce and Yeats have contributed to English literature. Surrounded by a group of eager fellow-workers, such as Indiana University, for instance, possesses, the chairman of the Curriculum can coordinate his program, offer supplementary seminars on problems, methods, scope and bibliog-raphy of Comparative Literature, and work out the requirements for an M. A. or a Ph. D. program in this fascinating field. In such a Curric-ulum, at least and at last, you have comradeship between the various departments in the Humanities, a happy cooperation, in lieu of the indifference or indeed the enmity or the snobbishness that exist, alas, in ever so many universities.

And what are the requirements for a degree in our field? Here I would take Indiana and Yale as the two extremes, with North Carolina, Wisconsin and Berkeley occupying what I would like to call a sound middle ground. Indiana, besides greatly stressing its graduate program, is especially known for favoring undergraduates' acquiring their B. A. in Comparative Literature, and for its fifteen to twenty large annual class-room sections dealing with so-called World Literature in English translation. Yale, on the other hand, holds, and justifiably so, that Comparative Literature is definitely not for undergraduates (who should first acquire their tools by majoring in one or more foreign languages and literatures), and that, in fact, Comparative Literature is even too hard and too advanced for M. A. candidates—and so Yale offers nothing but a Ph. D. program to the cream of the cream among its students. We at North Carolina certainly do not encourage undergraduates, and we may actually have five to eight B. A.'s per year; but we do push our graduate program, and at present we have more than thirty graduate comparatists working for either their M. A. or their Ph. D. It is to these young people that we give our full attention, and not to the under-graduates who, as a start, would be better off in a Greek, Spanish, Ger-man or Russian Department. The requirements for a Ph. D. are on the average 24 three-hour per week courses after the B. A., of which six courses each must be taken in three individual literature departments, while the fourth group of six courses must deal with distinctly comparative courses and seminars — and (the only work which the candidate is permitted to take in English translation) with about two courses on the Greek and Latin heritage of Western literature.[3] Our young Ph. D. thus knows three literatures in the original, and he usually chooses the period from the Renaissance to the present — though in the past few years we have also given two Ph. D.'s in medieval Comparative Literature, with modern literatures merely as a minor. If one of the three literatures is English, it means that he has to master only two foreign languages and literatures; if he is a patriotic American, it also means, if he so chooses, that he may cover English literature only from Chaucer to the deaths of Shelley and Byron, and that for the past 140 years he can switch over to American literature from Bryant to Faulkner, instead of taking in the Victorians and the twentieth century British writers. Yet another possible combination is one ancient and two modern literatures, *e.g.* Greek, Italian, and English. Our most frequent combination, however, has always been English, French, German.

A word of warning to those among us comparatists who may not find all the help needed on their campus and who, therefore, may have to teach most of the comparative courses themselves. That was the case with us at North Carolina where, before 1963, only a few among our colleagues in English, French or Spanish were able or willing to give courses on the vast influence of their golden ages upon neighboring literatures. Our students, therefore, have to take most of their three literatures straight, isolated, hermetically sealed from one another — and it is left to a mere handful of comparatists to build bridges and to point to the many crossfertilizations that occur among national literatures. We are, therefore, the sole Foreign Office in our Literature Division, and in our courses we stick to comparatism plain and simple. We would not wish to encroach upon other departments by analyzing *à fond* Dante, Shakespeare, Schiller or Whitman; instead, we dwell on what Dante received from Virgil and gave to Milton; how Shakespeare learned from

---

[3]Our most recent requirements at North Carolina have changed that to 7-6-5 courses in three literatures, and six comparative courses.

Ovid or Bandello, was abominated by Voltaire and hailed by Baretti and Goethe; what Schiller meant to the French romantic dramatists, and how Whitman, far more than Cooper or even Poe, was the first American to reverse the prevailing one-way traffic of literary influences from Europe to America, by casting mighty waves back upon Europe. Years of valuable experience in mobilizing the American comparatists into a solid organization within the Modern Language Association, an effort which culminated in the founding of our own journal, the publication of the *Bibliography* and the *Yearbooks*, and the founding of the International Comparative Literature Association,[4] have taught me that we are by no means welcome if, on our way up, instead of dwelling on foreign relations alone, we trespass upon the privileges of our colleagues in the various literature departments by telling them to move over, because we now want to do much of their work. That is the wrong approach, for we should do only what our colleagues cannot or will not do because of their own specializations and limitations. I have always been worried by the suggestion that all our titles, professors of English, French, German. or indeed of Comparative Literature, should be abolished, and that we all should just be called Professors of Literature, because many idealists maintain that it should be our task to consider a great masterpiece, *e.g. Don Quijote*, under all its various aspects, national as well as international. Such universally knowledgeable professors of Literature (with a capital L) died out long ago, and we all must be content with being mere specialists in one field or another. For my part, I have always been content to leave minute analyses of *De rerum natura*, *Paradise Lost*, *Wilhelm Meister* or *The Brothers Karamazov* in the hands of far better qualified specialists, and to be content with pointing to certain international ramifications of these works. That self-imposed restraint alone will make us acceptable and accepted on every campus, a friend and valued ally and supplementary coordinator, rather than a

---

[4]The various ICLA Congresses took place in Venice (1955), Chapel Hill (1958), Utrecht (1961), Fribourg (1964) and Belgrade (1967); and the Presidents of ICLA were J. -M. Carré (Sorbonne), C. Pellegrini (Firenze), M. Bataillon (Collège de France), W. P. Friederich (North Carolina), W. A. P. Smit (Utrecht), R. Wellek (Yale), R. Shackleton (Oxford), and J. Voisine (Sorbonne).

rival, in our common task of exploring the wonder of a great man or masterpiece in all directions.

In conclusion, a brief discussion of two outstanding American traits favoring Comparative Literature—traits of which, unfortunately, we can share only one with Australia. The one which we cannot share with you is our favorable geographical location at the very crossroads of events. Seven years ago I dwelled on the very promising future of American Comparatism in an address which I gave at the University of Zürich and which was subsequently published in Tübingen[5]—when I thought I should explain why, in our field, America had more than caught up with the leadership of France. When Paul van Tieghem in his *La Littérature comparée* stressed so much the role of intermediaries, he was thinking of little countries like Belgium, Switzerland and Czechoslovakia, indeed perhaps even of Alsace or of Austria, as ideal intermediaries between the Latin, the Germanic and the Slavic cultures of Europe. The United States, at that time, seemed far away, peripheral, unimportant in that Europe-centered view of things. Today it is different, for the U. S. are in the very hub of developments, not only in politics or science, but also in the great literary currents that move across oceans. Latin America, which used to be exposed directly to European cultural influences, now channels many of these by way of New York or Washington, for with the appearance of Franco in Spain, the once formidable bonds of "hispanidad" between Spain and Chile or Uruguay became loosened—entirely apart from the fact that the homeland of Whitman, Jack London or Hemingway became itself an increasingly important emittor. With regard to a Japan opened up to Western influences only a hundred years ago, it is again the United States that have become the land of the middle, passing on its own and general European literature at an accelerating speed since the victory and the occupation of 1945. As far as Australasia is concerned, and perhaps also other Commenwealth countries like India, with rich cultural possibilities and pitifully inadequate military means: the Suez crisis of less than

[5] Cf. p. 3 above, footnote 2

ten years ago has shown that the tenuous link with Europe, always at the mercy of Nasser, is very insecure indeed and that, in view of the powderkeg that is South Africa, the safest and most helpful road from London to Singapore or Christchurch may well lead by way of San Francisco. No—North America today is no longer merely peripheral, a continent tucked away between two immense oceans; for better or for worse, for Harvard as well as for Hollywood, it is, because of both its geography and its power, a first class emittor and intermediary.

A second trait, the one we can share with you and which fills me with great hope for a real beginning of Comparative Literature in Australia and a later blossoming (which insular England, for all its proximity to the great European mother-continent, may never experience) is the multi-racial background of the American and now also of the Australian peoples. Today there is hardly an American who does not have a couple of French, German, Swedish, Italian, Czech or Jewish ancestors—and Australia, likewise, has been so enormously enriched since 1945 by an influx of all sorts of national and racial elements that the beneficent impact has increasingly replaced a narrowly restrictive provincialism of attitude by a broader and more tolerantly cosmopolitan outlook on life and literature. The most unworthy among the European compara-tists, alas, often embraced this profession only to betray it, to ignore the fact that comparatism, in its last analysis, constitutes a political creed, an abjuring all of forms of racism—because, at times, these men publish so-called comparative books only to underscore all the more bigotedly the alleged superiority of their own national literature. Not so the Americans of today or the Australians of tomorrow, who can look back upon a richly varied ancestry and who have no special axe to grind —and for all their English mother-tongue, they will be fair and unbiased in weighing the literary debits and credits of the lands of their various ancestors. This may also make our students better linguists and better comparatists—and a mere glance at some of our leading comparatists in America will convince you that the work of Anglo-Saxons like Lawrence Marsden Price at Berkeley, Gilbert Highet at Columbia, Chandler Beall

48

at Oregon, Haskell Block at Brooklyn College,[6] Owen Aldridge at Maryland[7] or David Malone[8] at Southern California is more than amply supplemented by Frenchmen like Henri Peyre at Yale or Gilbert Chinard at Princeton, by Germans like Horst Frenz[9] at Indiana, Victor Lange at Princeton or Oskar Seidlin[10] at Ohio State, by Italians like Gian Orsini at Wisconsin or Giuseppe Fucilla at Northwestern, by Czechs like René Wellek at Yale, Swiss like François Jost at Illinois, Spaniards like José de Onís at Colorado, Poles like Zbigniew Folejewski at Pennsylvania, Russians like Gleb Struve at Berkeley. This same inspiring wealth can be seen among the literary figures of America, too—from the French background of Philippe Freneau in the days of Jefferson to the German background of Theodore Dreiser, the Portuguese ancestry of John Dos Passos, the pure Anglo-Saxonism of Robert Frost, the Armenian traits in William Saroyan, the Jewish roots of Shalom Asch, the Italian heritage of Frances Winwar, alias Francesca Vinciguerra, the rich Negro vein in Langston Hughes, Richard Wright and James Baldwin.

And, speaking of these colored Americans—at moments when we are all deeply depressed by what occurred in Little Rock or in Birmingham, let us never forget, happily and perhaps a bit proudly, that the voice of the Black Man was heard for the first time in history not in Africa, not on the shores of the Congo, but on the shores of the Mississippi—and that it was in ever upward-struggling America that the former slaves, in moving spirituals, in gripping novels, dramas or poems, were first given a chance to give expression to their hopes and their anguish, to

---

[6]Founder of the American Comparative Literature Association. It was entirely due to Mr. Block's admirable energy and farsightedness that it was possible to establish an ACLA independent of the Modern Language Association of America. This forceful new organization which, of course, works in close co-operation with the ICLA, held its first congresses at Columbia University (1962), Harvard University (1965) and Indiana University (1968) and its first presidents were W. P. Friederich, René Wellek, Harry Levin and Chandler Beall.

[7]Editor of the *Comparative Literature Studies*, Maryland 1963/64; now at the University of Illinois.

[8]Chairman at U.S.C., and prime mover of the distinguished Pacific Coast Comparative Literature Symposia.

[9]Since 1961 Editor of the *Yearbook of Comparative and General Literature*.

[10]Co-editor of *Arcadia, Zeitschrift für vergleichende Literaturwissenschaft* (de Gruyter, Berlin).

the despair and the vision of a race that is justly aspiring to a respected place on earth.

All this is our life's blood, the vast province which we comparatists can explore, the challenge which we can meet and overcome when we are frustrated and discouraged by the narrowness of ever so much in merely nationally conceived literary scholarship. I should like to conclude with a statement by Ralph Waldo Emerson against an anti-foreign political party of more than 100 years ago which seems particularly fitting in the connection: "I hate the narrowness of the Native American Party", Emerson says in his *Journal* of September 1845. "It is the dog in the manger. It is precisely opposite to all the dictates of love and magnanimity; and therefore, of course, opposite to true wisdom... Man is the most composite of all creatures... As in the old burning of the Temple of Corinth, by the melting and intermixture of silver and gold and other metals, a new compound more precious than any, called the Corinthian brass, was formed; so in this continent — asylum of all nations — the energy of Irish, Germans, Swedes, Poles and Cossacks, and all the European tribes, — of the Africans, and of the Polynesians, — will construct a new race, a new religion, a new state, a new literature, which will be as vigorous as the new Europe which came out of the melting-pot of the Dark Ages... La Nature aime les croisements."

What Emerson said about the America of the 1850's can likewise be said about the Australia of the 1960's — and it is this kind of thinking that almost induces me, a man of three fatherlands as it were, Switzerland, the United States and Australia, to dedicate this rather hopeful talk on "The Challenge of Comparative Literature" to the New Australians among you. For yours is a great opportunity indeed.

VI. ON THE HUMANIZING INFLUENCE OF LITERATURE[1]

Dante, in the fifth canto of his *Inferno*, when speaking of the famous illicit lovers Paolo and Francesca da Rimini, inserts the somber, contemplative line of "Nessun maggior dolore...", that there is no greater grief than, in times of misfortune, to remember past happiness.

All of you might take these words as a motto for your present life —for, regardless of whether you are rich or poor, bright or average, you are all in the promising life-building phase of your earthly existence. Your success, good fortune, wealth, power or indeed happiness are not so much acquired twenty or thirty years from now; the foundation for all this is being laid right now, while you are here in Chapel Hill. It all depends on how well you use the four years a kindly fate or the sacrifices of your parents have bestowed upon you at this college —whether you strengthen your character and widen your intellectual horizon, or whether you waste your time and, cockily, keep on looking for and following the path of least resistance. Forty years from now, when your career is over and you find yourselves in some groove of mediocrity, misfortune, eternal discontent and self-reproaches, you, too, may remember past happiness, past chances, past unfulfilled promises.

Thus the time is the here and the now; no alibis and no glib assertions to the contrary can fool you about this fact. It is a beautiful time of golden opportunities—but also a dangerous time. If you do not believe me and if you need a real shocker, go to the Bowery in New York and watch all the drunks in the gutter in broad daylight—not only tramps and bums, but some, once upon a time, students, officers, lawyers,

[1]Address to undergraduate students of the Di-Phi Senate, University of North Carolina, October 1963.

salesmen of sorts who have failed to take advantage of their chances and who, at some critical and deeply tragic moment of their lives, had completely let go of themselves, their jobs and families. In the half-darkness of their present existence they, too, may agonize over the words of Francesca da Rimini.

If, as professor of literature, I beg you to keep on everlastingly reading books, good books, fiction, drama, history, biography, it is not to proselytize and make students of literature out of all of you. You are welcome to become scientists, engineers, physicians, lawyers, business tycoons — we need all of them. I do not share present fears that the world is going to the dogs because scientists instead of humanists begin to prevail among us — and if you ever hear a humanist accuse a scientist of being a less well-rounded person, turn the spear around by asking the former just how much of the sciences he has studied and retained. The chances are, mighty little. But I would beg all of you, at this critical moment of your lives, as you prepare yourselves for a career in business or science, never to forget your common cultural heritage with the humanists, your common humanity, the need to be decent, socially, politically and philosophically sane human beings among your fellow-men.

The early acquired habit of reading good books alone can fully humanize you and keep you from becoming mere adding-machines or spiritually stunted laboratory-experimenters. And this is because, alas, in the turmoil of our mechanized civilization, great fiction and great biography alone still dwell extensively on the sanctity of the human heart, the dignity of all human existence. For many of our friends, the sociologists, we all do not exist as individuals any longer. Gone is the day of the small community, the compact cultural unit, of individual prowess, when everybody knew everybody else, as you still have in Homer's *Iliad*, or as I still encountered on small, compact islands like Tasmania, where the individual and his clan still counted for something. Instead, we now count people by the millions and by the billions — and the individual has disappeared, has become a mere cipher. Today, we are evaluated only as multiple categories — so many male, so many female; so many white, so many colored; so many under 21, so many over 65; so many white-collar workers, so many laborers—"percentagewise" this and "percentagewise" that. As students you receive a number; as soldiers you are a mere number. We have our social security number; now we even have checking-account numbers, zip-code numbers—all of us just a vast, grey, enormous, yet numbered mass of people. The FBI has millions of our fingerprints (as if that were really us!)—and, no doubt, in hospitals and in death we will have different numbers again.

Great literature alone opposes itself to that pernicious, personality-killing trend. In great books alone do you find—not the supremacy of the masses, but the importance of the individual. Volumes of lyric poems continue to be written about that innermost part of our own selves which the statisticians never reach: our heart, our soul, our mind, our ecstasy—sonnets, odes, dithyrambs, about what God or love or the beauties of nature mean to us—to you and me, personally, not just to the Class of 1966 as a whole, or the inhabitants of the Western Hemisphere as a whole. Hundreds of volumes of fiction, from Cervantes to Fielding, Tolstoy and Proust have been written, and continue to be written, about the hopes, dreams and frustrations of individual human beings, all of them and their emotions analyzed, probed and respected for their own sake—lovingly, respectfully, devotedly, as though the individual human being still counted for something, as though he still were what some of us always thought he should be, the nearest thing to God on earth. Or take again the vast field of the drama, the outstanding tragedies of man's confrontation with Fate or with moments of heroic greatness: they cannot fail to imbue us with pride and reassurance about our own otherwise insignificant selves, whether they deal with the death of Antigone or the Death of a Salesman.

This re-assurance we all need—of our own dignity, individual importance, potential divinity. If you don't believe me and are satisfied being a soulless cog in a soulless machine, read George Orwell's *1984*, where man indeed has lost his humaneness and his divine spark.

There are other reasons why you should read, at all times. Good books alone help you to keep your sanity and your sense of proportion. You need them most of all in the great crises in your own personal lives—crises which none of you will be spared. Unwise people, alas, who have no sense of proportion and comparison, take themselves far too seriously and are apt to behave in a shamelessly unbridled fashion. With their dull wits they imagine that nobody has ever quite loved or hated as they have, been double-crossed or deserted or maligned—and in blind fury they strike out against the alleged wrong-doer, and another one of the numberless crimes recorded by the statisticians has been committed. The truly educated man, however, agrees with Montaigne that he reads in order to learn to live, in order to learn to know others and his own self, indeed, in order to learn to suffer and die with dignity. No matter what may happen to him—through his readings he knows that the same thing, or worse, has happened to thousands of others; that the moment calls for fortitude, and not despair; that the crisis, the tragedy in his life, calls for moral re-assertion and, if possible, greatness, and not for frothing mouths and cheap spectacles. Moderation, humility, and a true sense of relativity—these surely are not among the least welcome concomitants of the humanizing influence of great literature upon us.

I can give you only a few hints concerning the hundreds of good books you should choose from, now and in the future, whenever your day is done and you have a few hours for peace and meditation, with the inane sportspages and funnies of the rest of your family thrown down into the cellar and with the frequently equally unworthy radios and television sets turned off. First, read the literature of any so-called Enemy. Do not condemn an entire people for political reasons before taking the trouble of acquainting yourselves with some outstanding cultural achievements of that people. Your parents, in their splendid isolation and selfrighteousness (to find forgiving words for what they did), sinned by referring to "Limies", "Wops" and "Frogs", by ostracizing the music of Wagner as well as the poetry of Goethe, just because of deep-seated political, rather than more tolerant cultural, attitudes. Try not to emulate their self-defeating shortsightedness as you face the very grave political uncertainties of the 1960's; try to appreciate not only the music of Tchaikovsky or the old novels by Dostoevsky, but perhaps even modern prose epics by Mikhail Sholokhov—no matter how detestable his personal lack of integrity—such as *The Don Flows Home to The Sea* or *Seeds of Tomorrow,* in order to grasp what exactly drove the Russians to the great Revolution of 1917 or to the establishment of agricultural communes. I do not fear for a moment that these novels will corrupt you; the desperate human plights described therein will appeal to you, the cruelty, wholsesale killing and sheer stupidity of the events will repel you—and in the end you will thank God for living in America. But at least you will have made an honest effort to understand what makes the modern Russians tick—and, mortal enemy of their system though you will be, you will never quite hate and condemn as blindly as the McCarthyites did in the 1950's, and as the present lunatic fringe does.

Second, during the present tragic age of national crisis, of a veritable new American Revolution, of the deep significance of which I am afraid most of you are but dimly and indifferently aware: read the literature, the testimonies, the outcries of the Black Man. Be proud, if you can, that the voice of the Negro, for the first time in human history appeared right here in America, and that, since the end of the eighteenth century, he has added, timidly at first, submissively, unsure of himself, but ever more boldly later, his voice to the voices of Anglo-Saxons, Spaniards, Irishmen, Scandinavians, Frenchmen, Germans, that have contributed to the greatness not only of American literature, but to the greatness of the political dream that is America. Try to understand what is moving his heart and his hopes and read his lyrical poems, like the one by James Corrothers:

> To be a Negro in a day like this -
> Alas, Lord God, what evil have we done?

or another one, by Langston Hughes, proudly asserting himself as a human being among other human beings, a bit resembling Walt Whitman's "Song of Myself", and ending

> I, too, am America!

in order to understand the history of generations of suffering, oppression, man's inhumanity to man, and yet also of hope and faith—faith not only in an Old Testament God who sent Moses to "go and tell old Pharaoh to let My people go", but faith also in the ultimate sense of justice and of fair play among the vast majority of the American people. Or read stark, naturalistic and despairing novels like Richard Wright's *Native Son*, and marvel anew, if your soul is big enough, at the deep-seated loyalty of the American Negro, and his innate strength in refusing to be ensnared by Communist propaganda. Yes, read Negro literature by all means and learn thereby in God's good time to solve a problem which your parents could not and would not solve—and do not forget that the only two saintly men our poor twentieth century has produced, the late Mahatma Gandhi in India and Albert Schweitzer in darkest Africa, will bless you for your honest attempt at understanding, mitigating and helping. Or, if some of you, in your daily lives making a mockery of Him who died on the cross for preaching decency and good will, prefer the voice of harshness to the voice of goodness in order to be converted: be deeply hurt and angrily perplexed by an assertion made about three weeks ago by the noted anti-American British philosopher Bertrand Russell who said that America, in the last 350 years, had committed more crimes of murder, flogging, rape and exploitation against the Negro than Hitler had with the more than six million known victims of National Socialism. It is of no use to cry out in shame and dismay that the British lord is a liar, that surely this cannot be so—for the word has been spoken and, right or wrong, it has hit its mark, it has hit all of us, all Americans, the living and the dead. And if it has been dinned into the ears of the German people for the past twenty years that they all, all of them, are collectively guilty, that they all must atone, repent and expiate until Doomsday—just where do guilt and atonement begin and end for all of us?

And third and last, yet another category of books that should accompany you through life, from young manhood to old age: read both history and fiction, drama and essay about our own America—about the United States in general and the dignity and the integrity of the real flower of the Old South in particular. Perhaps you will share my profound admiration for my two favorite Americans—Roger Williams, the founder of seventeenth-century Rhode Island, for his political idealism and his religious tolerance, and Robert E. Lee, who revealed an even greater humaneness and patriotism in peace, in defeat, rather than in the war itself. Add to their shining examples some of Emerson's essays on the finest aspects of American faith and optimism, or study Francis Parkman's gripping description of the gigantic struggle between the French and the British-American claimants to this continent, a struggle between the Jesuit- and royalist-dominated system of absolutistic France and the far freer and nobler democratic traditions of the Anglo-Americans to realize what this country fought for, what dreams of justice and dignity it had, and what still remains unfulfilled among those dreams. Or, in the field of the drama – what better reformulation of innate strength, wisdom and ultimate victory in times of grave crises could there be than in Maxwell Anderson's *Valley Forge*, in Sidney Kingsley's *The Patriots*, or indeed in Robert Sherwood's *Abe Lincoln in Illinois?* These were high enough ideals to live up to when the United States was an outsider in world politics, squeezed in between the Atlantic and the Alleghenies, or the Atlantic and the Rockies; now that she has become the leader and the hope of the entire Free World, you, the young generation, must feel almost crushed by the heavy responsibility of letting no major taint, weakness or innate unworthiness ever soil the image of America's strength and basic decency.

And, in conclusion, to turn from international and even national politics to rather local tasks and responsibilities of our young intellectuals humanized by the study of history and of literature; after you have become aware again of the finest aspects of southern thinking from Jefferson and Madison to Lee and beyond, you will, I hope, regain a new respect for the dignity of the Confederate flag – the symbol of a lost cause, but the symbol, too, under which tens of thousands of men fought and died. If you think you really *must* revive the memory of the Confederate flag at his moment when Civil Rights for all are on the verge of being acknowledged, I should say that this flag belongs in your hearts and shrines, a memento of what men lived and died for, a symbol, perhaps, for a quiet and meditative procession on the anniversary of Appomattox. It must not – as alas, it has, in recent months and years

—become defiled and prostituted by screaming mobs in Alabama, Mississippi and elsewhere, out to terrorize the population, to insult the high office of the Presidency of the United States, or to impeach members of the Supreme Court. That is not what the Confederate flag is here for; it is not the equivalent of a pirate's skull and crossbones—and Robert E. Lee would turn in his grave if he knew what was being perpetrated in his name. The flag of my own little native country, Switzerland, the white cross in the red field, in the course of generations became sublimated and ennobled into something much bigger and finer, namely the Red Cross in the white field—for Switzerland was the first to establish that great humanitarian and international organization to alleviate suffering all over the world. In that form the inverted flag of Switzerland, the Red Cross, will live on and on, long after the country of its origin has been absorbed in the coming United States of Europe. I hope and pray that you will help to restore your Confederate flag to its former place of respect and piety—and I invite you to strive for a similar sublimation of its meaning to the one that occurred in the case of the Swiss flag.

PART TWO

VII. THE COSMOPOLITANISM AND OTHER TRAITS OF SWISS LITERATURE[1]

If in your deliberations on the quintessence of Comparative Literature you have followed the booklet of the venerable Paul van Tieghem, *La Littérature comparée*, you have seen how much importance the French attach to intermediaries — nations as intermediaries, like Holland between the Anglo-German and French block, or Czechoslovakia between the Teuton and the Slav; entire groups as intermediaries, such as refugees like the Huguenots or the White Russians, and the salons of eighteenth-century France; individuals as intermediaries, such as travellers or translators. Do not ever let anybody convince you that intermediaries are unimportant, engaged only in international literary commerce. Of course, like the best of ideas, their investigation can be cheapened by a purely mechanical procedure which lacks aesthetic evaluation, when statistically-minded compilers mechanically count all the translations of, and the books and articles about, Zola or James Joyce abroad and then present the final result of their work on vast statistical charts, as a stock-broker would do with regard to the rise or the fall of a certain stock. Such a prodecure is hardly satisfactory, for it completely leaves out a probing analysis *e.g.* of *Ulysses* as a work of art, and it also reduces the researcher's own evaluative and interpretative skills to the barest minimum.

With regard to our topic of today, the presentation of the role and the general cultural and historical background of an intermediary, let us begin with quite a few general facts and chief characteristics of Swiss

[1]Paper read at Indiana University in 1963, basically a compilation from various earlier articles: "Chief Traits of Swiss Literature," *South Atlantic Quarterly*, XLVII, 1948, 173-85; "Some Aspects of Switzerland's Significance During the Renaissance," *Straumann Festschrift, English Studies*, XLIII, 1962, 319-23, etc.

literature before coming to the heart of our topic, the problem particularly dear to any student of Comparative Literature: the intermediary
role of Switzerland, especially during the Renaissance, and during the
eighteenth and the first half of the nineteenth centuries.

By way of general information: of the five million Swiss, seventy
per cent speak German, twenty-two per cent French, seven per cent
Italian, and one per cent, the inhabitants of some valleys in the Grisons,
speak Romansh. Thus, there *is* no national Swiss language; the best
German-Swiss authors, from today's Friedrich Dürrenmatt to earlier
centuries, are usually included in the histories of German literature,
just as, for an earlier period, Rousseau and Mme de Staël, both from
Geneva, are always included in the histories of French literature. Yet,
in spite of this disadvantage, it is plausible to contend with Emil Ermatinger in his basically important *Dichtung und Geistesleben der deutschen
Schweiz* that there is a specifically Swiss spirit, and hence a specifically
Swiss literature which exists regardless of the rather unimportant differences of languages. Switzerland is the exception among the peoples:
she is a compact nation held together not by common language, race
or religion, but by common ideals, and by the memory of centuries of
common struggle in defense of her liberties. This bond of political
freedom and true internal democracy is stronger than the bond of blood
or language that might attract the German-Swiss to Germany, the
French-Swiss to France, or the Italian-Swiss to Italy. Berlin and Paris,
Rome and Vienna, will always remain highly respected cultural centers
from which the Swiss will gladly learn; but in case of doubts and inner
conflicts, these foreign influences will shatter against 670 years of common history, against centuries of living together and believing together
in the noble goals of the old confederacy of 1291. Switzerland is thus
not a racial or even a cultural unity, but solely a political idea held together by mutual faith, tolerance and democracy – a state in which
suspicions, recriminations and bad will cannot exist, because with these
the state and the ideal would cease to exist.

We can afford to single out only three chief traits in this literature,
largely German-Swiss and French-Swiss, for Italian-Swiss and Romansh
literatures began to become really noticeable only from the nineteenth

century on. First, lyrical poetry (with the exception of Keller and Meyer in Zürich) does not flourish and, worse, up to a few years ago, one could also have said that the drama is practically nonexistent – except for Friedrich Dürrenmatt and Max Frisch, whose dramas have suddenly appeared on the contemporary scene, totally unexpectedly and, one might almost say, inexplicably. That leaves only the novel – a genre in which Swiss writers excel. In novels and essays and political, religious and pedagogical treatises the sober Swiss best express their maturely considered, somewhat heavy, and always didactic ideas. Beauty for beauty's sake does not exist with them; always the *delectare* is closely coupled with the *prodesse*, and a book must have some ultimate purpose to justify its existence. Moreover, this sober literature of Switzerland eschews excesses. French Switzerland, to be sure, had two moderately romantic writers, Mme de Staël and Benjamin Constant; but apart from these, Romanticism is alien to Swiss mentality. German-Swiss authors, Muralt, Haller, Gessner and Bodmer were among the foremost leaders of Europe, around 1740, in bringing about the downfall of French Classicism, and in conjuring up the dawn of an ardent and irrational Pre-Romanticism; but with the beginning of Romanticism itself, and its many excesses, the Swiss voices broke off. Again, around 1850, Swiss literature through Gotthelf, Keller and Meyer produced some of the finest masterpieces of European Realism; but when that Realism degenerated into Naturalism, when faultfinding and the quest of the malodorous became the chief purpose of literature, the Swiss refused to follow suit. There is not a single Swiss naturalist of consequence unless, again, we except the weird mixture of Symbolism and Naturalism of our unexpected contemporaries Dürrenmatt and Frisch, for this land of moderate wealth and of social justice saw no need to undermine the solidity of the state. Instead, with sobriety and patriotism, one turned to useful, to constructive things – and it is not sheer coincidence that Switzerland gave to Europe two of its best-known writers on education, Jean-Jacques Rousseau and Heinrich Pestalozzi; that she gave to German-speaking lands one of the earliest great historians, who came decades ahead of the Treitschkes and the Rankes, Johannes von Müller; and that she gave to the Western World one of the finest

63

"Kulturhistoriker", Jakob Burckhardt. That, rather than romantic unbridledness or naturalistic muckraking, seemed a worthwhile activity.

A second important trait is the Swiss authors' love of nature, emphatic, often deeply moving, and entirely comprehensible in view of the serene beauty, the majesty, the awe-inspiring greatness of the Alps, of the glaciers, the lakes, the valleys, the flora of Switzerland. Generalizing rather broadly, we can say that the entire eighteenth century in Europe indicated a growing rebellion against the system of Versailles, against the society, the corruption of the *Ancien Régime*, against the petrified lifelessness of Neo-Classicism—and that the poets after 1740 demanded nature instead of civilization, ardor instead of skepticism, vigorous originality instead of dry imitation. It is natural that the Swiss writers of that age should have been among the harbingers of Pre-Romanticism, for Switzerland was in every respect the antithesis of Versailles, and that the French-Swiss and the German-Swiss authors should have vied with one another in praising the beauties of the Alps and in extolling the simple virtues of the God-fearing mountaineers. In a century which yearned for the Golden Age of Innocence, Albrecht von Haller and Jean-Jacques Rousseau were naively sure that this fabulous age could still be found in the Swiss mountains, far away from the corruption of big cities, of demoralized courts, and of a decadent civilization. Haller's famous poem *Die Alpen* (1729) was intensely ardent and patriotic, one of the first works to preach a return to nature; and Rousseau's celebrated novel *Julie, ou la Nouvelle Héloïse* likewise placed the earthly paradise of the two as yet happily uninhibited lovers in Switzerland, on the shores of Lake Geneva, near Vevey. More healthily skeptical were Salomon Gessner and Johann Rudolf Wyss in their search for, and description of, the long lost Golden Age of Innocence, for Gessner, the most famous idyllic writer of his century, placed his *Idylle* in a faraway biblical time, when sin did not yet exist and when Cain had not yet slain Abel; and Wyss in his later *Der schweizerische Robinson*, written during the height of the Napoleonic Wars, sought the peace which he could no longer find in French-invaded Switzerland somewhere on a lonely island beyond Africa. Yet love of the Alpine regions remained one of the great driving forces of Swiss writers, from Jeremias Gotthelf,

64

the creator of the peasant or regional novel in early nineteenth century German-Swiss literature, to Charles-Ferdinand Ramuz in early twentieth-century French-Swiss literature.

Yet another, a third significant trait of Swiss literature is its constant political purposefulness, its constant emphasis on the interest of the community, on political and social amelioration. With their strongly didactic vein, the Swiss are habitual believers in enlightenment; they rarely neglect a chance to derive some profound, though perhaps soberly homespun, truth from a given situation. As early as 1657 Jakob von Graviseth (or was it Hans Franz Veiras?) wrote a moralizing and critical work describing an imaginary trip through some imaginary land called *Heutelia* (an anagram, of course, of Helvetia or Switzerland), in which he subjected social, political and religious shortcomings to a close scrutiny. The book was published at least half a century before the Age of Enlightenment began on the Continent, at least two generations before Montesquieu in his equally well-disguised *Lettres persanes* undertook a similarly critical trip through France. Then came Rousseau, erroneously called a Frenchman by most people; yet the very fact that he was born and bred in Switzerland made him a great and utterly indigestible rebel in France, as the recent and impressive two-volume work by our colleague François Jost shows. He was a Protestant among Catholics, a Genevan among Parisians, a plebeian among aristocrats, a republican among monarchists, a romanticist among classicists. Just as the eulogy of the Alps in *La Nouvelle Héloïse* could not have been written by anyone but a Swiss, so *Le contrat social* is a glorification of a democratic and republican form of government — not as it actually existed in Geneva, but as it should have existed there in the eyes of that patriotic citizen. Equally earnest in its petit-bourgeois spartanism is Rousseau's well-known *Lettre à d'Alembert sur les spectacles*, in a way the most Swiss of all his works, an essay in which he emphatically protests against Voltaire's plan to have a theatre established in Geneva. Here he scornfully refers to the French as "they" — a nation with immoral dramas, loose-living actors and actresses, with shallow and unworthy principles; a nation that would not dare to disturb the innocence, the peace, the Calvinistic austerity, the virtuous and wholesome amusements of the small Alpine republic. After Rousseau came Haller from Bern, in German Switzerland, writing in a different language, yet putting his shoulder to the same wheel, and fighting for the same cause. The grave Haller may have considered his lyrical poems of the type of his *Die Alpen* ephemeral pastimes of his youth; but in his old age he wrote three heavy state-novels, veritable testaments of his political thought. The most important of these was *Fabius und Cato* of 1774, in which Haller identified himself completely with the stern Cato, speaking up for a small Spartan democracy and warning against imperialism, dictatorship, and immoral contamination by debauched foreign nations – the Roman Cato thereby meaning the Orient, but the Swiss Haller thereby alluding to the declining moral rectitude of the France of Louis XV. Then came Johannes von Müller, the historian, whose *Geschichten der schweizerischen Eidgenossenschaften* were again a constant lecture in praise of old Swiss simplicity, strength, virtue, unity and democracy – tragically enough begun but a few years before the Confederacy, in 1798, for the only time in almost seven centuries, had to endure a foreign, a French, invasion and occupation.

I think I have said enough to indicate at least some of the basic trends in Swiss literature – and we can now discuss what to me is the most thoroughly fascinating aspect of Swiss intellectual life: namely her role as an intermediary between nations, her importance as *Helvetia mediatrix*, as Fritz Ernst, the late comparatist in Zürich, so felicitously called her in his excellent book on *Die Schweiz als geistige Mittlerin*, which I would love to have written myself. Switzerland indeed displays a strongly cosmopolitan trend. Situated on the roof of Europe, at the crossroads of three of the greatest of its modern cultures, and *eo ipso* part of them, Switzerland is not a barrier between Germany, France and Italy; rather, she is a bridge between them, a clearing-house for all men of goodwill. The most varied clouds may drift over Europe and finally settle over the Alps and empty themselves, filling the lakes and rivers of Switzerland – and she (to use an image suggested by Ermatinger), like one of the scores of little mountain lakes, gathers these waters, filters them, and carries the best that is in them into the valleys and among the neighboring countries below: through the Rhine into

Germany and the North Sea; through the Rhone into France and the Mediterranean; through the Ticino into the Po, into Italy and the Adriatic; through the Inn River in the Engadin into the Danube, the Balkans, the Black Sea. In times of peace Switzerland is a God-sent transmitter of all that is good, acknowledging no borders, no chauvinistic intolerance in her task of mediating among nations; in times of war she is a reservoir, almost a museum, a guardian of Western culture, preserving it until a Europe restored to its senses can use these treasures again.

I am choosing the sixteenth century of Zwingli's Reformation in Zürich and in about two-thirds of the Swiss cantons to show how Switzerland as a country, rather than its literature only, was able to serve as an important intermediary and shelter. Though the country was soon torn by religious dissensions, and though the Protestant defeat and Zwingli's death in 1531 enabled the Catholic cantons to retain the real authority in this predominantly Protestant nation, Switzerland nevertheless managed to become an important shelter for religious and political refugees from abroad. We need not refer so much to the obvious example, Jean Calvin, a French refugee who certainly made good in Geneva—nor, in a more deeply tragic sense, to Ulrich von Hutten who, hunted down by Church and Empire, died miserably on the Ufenau, the refuge Zwingli had generously provided for him. Italian refugees included the powerful Franciscan orator, Bernardino Ochino, who came to Geneva after the teachings of Luther and Erasmus had turned him away from Rome, and who then went on to England, only to go back to Switzerland after Mary Tudor's ascent to the English throne in 1553 endangered his life. Among other Italians in Geneva was the Diodati family which later was to become important because of Giovanni Diodati's translation of the *Bible* into Italian in 1603, and also because of Milton's later contacts with the family. Indeed, the Sismondi family, too, originally from Pisa, came by way of France to Geneva for reasons of faith. The only tragic exception among these refugees whom Switzerland failed completely in his hour of need was the Spanish humanist and physician, Michael Servetus, who, because of his anti-Trinitarianism, was burned at the stake in Calvin's Geneva in 1553.

67

The English Counter-Reformation under Mary Tudor, the wife of Philip II of Spain, naturally drove great numbers of English Protestant leaders to continental shelters in the Lowlands, in Germany, and in the Swiss cantons. Zürich under Zwingli's successor Heinrich Bullinger, Geneva under Calvin and his successor Théodore de Bèze (another Frenchman, a Burgundian, residing in Switzerland), and Basel were the three Swiss Protestant centers that took in the greatest number of these refugess until the death of "Bloody Mary" and the coming to power of Queen Elizabeth finally permitted them to return to their homeland. The history of the role of Zürich in this connection need not be repeated; in Geneva, besides the outstanding figure of the Scot John Knox, we might single out William Whittingham, an Englishman who stayed on and left behind a great work, begun and finally finished and printed there by a group of Englishmen during and after their years of exile, namely the *Geneva Bible* of 1560.

If we turn from the religious and political significance of Zürich and Geneva to the city of Basel, we notice at once that its importance was above all scholarly and humanistic, for Basel was the home of the oldest Swiss university which, alas, gave short shrift to the daringly new ideas of the first great physician of modern times, Paracelsus, a native of Schwyz. Basel, largely because of famous names like Frobenius and Oporinus, was also one of the first great and boldly unorthodox printing-centers of Europe; it was the temporary abode of artists like Hans Holbein—and, above all, it was the city in which Erasmus of Rotterdam, from 1521 on, spent longer and happier years than in any other city of Europe during his cosmopolitan life, and where he died in 1536. In view of Erasmus' close connections with Basel, it is not astonishing that his own *Epigrammata*, together with the *Epigrammata* and the second edition of the *Utopia* by Thomas Morus, should have been published by Frobenius in 1518, embellished by a woodcut by Holbein —and that the first complete edition of the Latin works of Thomas Morus should also have appeared there in 1563. Among the English refugees in Basel during the reign of Mary Tudor were John Foxe and John Bale—the latter a Protestant controversialist best known in English literature for his encyclopedic listing of all old and more recent English authors, which he published with Oporinus in 1559 under the title of *Scriptorum illustrium majoris Britanniae... catalogus.* John Foxe endured his years of exile by working as a proof-reader for Oporinus; it was his employer who published his religious drama *Christus triumphans* in 1556 and then, three years later, the first complete edition, in Latin, of his *Book of Martyrs*, of which the first English version appeared shortly after Foxe's return to London in 1563.

As an important Protestant printing center, Basel was greatly favored because, as the example of John Foxe shows, it made possible the printing of books which were frowned upon by the Catholic Church. To be sure, Zürich may be said to have begun this trend, for it is commonly agreed that Miles Coverdale's *Holy Scripture of the Olde and New Testament faithfully and newly translated out of the Doutche and Latyn into English* was printed there in 1535; but within one year Basel forged ahead when Calvin had his *Institutio religionis christianae* published there, even before he commenced his career in Geneva. The memory of Erasmus' link with Frobenius also lingered on among the many unorthodox Spanish "erasmistas", and it is not surprising that *Las ciento diez consideraciones divinas* by Juan de Valdés, suppressed by the Spanish Inquisition, should have been printed posthumously in Basel, rather than in the native Spain of the much-suspected author. Among texts from Italy, Oporinus produced in 1559 the *editio princeps* of Dante's *De Monarchia*, a work which had been unacceptable to Rome and to Catholic printers on account of its emphatically pro-Ghibelline and anti-papal viewpoint. Because of the desperate need of Protestants to look for potential allies even in the camp of the enemy, the Church of Rome, we need not marvel that Dante's theological and political treatise was at once translated by Johann Herold, (a former German who subsequently added Basilius to his name), under the title of *Die Monarchey, oder dass das Keyserthumb zu der wolfart diser Welt von nöten sey*, and published by Oporinus in the same year, 1559, more than two hundred years before Bachenschwanz supplied the Germans with their first translation of the *Divina Commedia*. Another minor example of Basel's serving as a greatly needed printing center for anti-catholic refugees can be seen in Matthias Flaccius Illyricus, a fervent Italian Lutheran, whose long and bitter catalogue of testimonies against the Roman Church and Roman errors appeared in 1556 under the title of *Catalogus testium veritatis qui ante nostram aetatem pontifici romano et papismi erroribus reclamarunt*. To turn to another "heresy": though the first Arabic book was published in Fano, Italy, in 1514, it seemed entirely natural that the first Latin translation of the *Koran* should appear in Basel, in 1543. On the other hand, however, her enviably independent position occasionally also brought Basel a loss, and not only gains—for instance when Sebastian Brant, professor of law at her university and well known for his famous satire *Das Narrenschiff*, left the city when it was on the point of deciding to detach itself from the Holy Roman Empire and to become a member of the Swiss Confederacy, and moved over into German Alsace instead.

Of far less importance than this beautiful role of refuge, printing center, and clearing-house in Europe's unending stream of Renaissance ideas were the reverberations of Switzerland's own scholars and institutions abroad. Great poets to influence the rest of Europe she had none; among her native intellectual leaders Zwingli was the only giant, the gentlest of all reformers if compared with Luther or Calvin, the only leader of the new faith still on good terms with the humanists. As to the true democracy of some rustic and some municipal cantons of Switzerland: the time for democracy and for Switzerland's leading role in its propagation was not to come for at least another two hundred years. And so what remains by way of foreign echoes is a couple of Swiss humanists who lived abroad, and a German epic, Johannes Fischart's *Das glückhaft' Schiff von Zürich*, 1577, eulogizing Swiss military preparedness.

To speak only of the humanists: one of them was Niklaus von Wyle, a lawyer from Aargau who died in Zürich in 1478 and who spent decades of his life as high administrative chancellor in Swabia. In Germany, he helped to rekindle the lamps of learning around 1450, after the Hussite Wars had extinguished the first promising beginnings of Humanism north of the Alps, in Bohemia. As a pioneer humanist of the fifteenth century, Wyle was especially active in translating Italian humanistic works into German, not only philosophical treatises like Petrarca's *De remediis utriusque fortunae*, but also some of the secular works of Boccaccio and of Poggio, and the amorous tale *Euryalus and Lucretia* (*De duobus amantibus*) by Aenea Silvio Piccolomini, later Pope Pius II. More significant was Joachim von Watt of St. Gallen, scientist, astronomer, poet and literary critic, who went to the Imperial Court in Vienna in 1502 and who, crowned poet by the Emperor in 1514 under the latinized name of Vadianus, is especially important for his *De poetica et carminis ratione*. These lectures, given at the University of Vienna in 1513 and printed five years later, present the first theory of literature to be issued in modern Europe, a first discussion of genres, themes, versification, with striking outlines of Greek and Roman literature, of the ecclesiastical and secular works of the Middle Ages, and even of the new Renaissance trends in Italian literature. Yet Watt's participation in the Protestant Revolt after his return to Switzerland in 1518 indicates how deeply rooted this international humanist was in the mentality and the aspirations of his people.

Switzerland was to play a possibly even greater role in European thought 200 years later. After the long French hegemony over Europe, the Swiss, early in the eighteenth century were the first to point to England, from which both the Age of the Enlightenment and of the Storm and Stress derived so much inspiration, and to translate and explain to continental readers the relatively unknown literature of that island. In the sixteenth it was the foreign guests in a passive and peaceful land that had attracted our attention; now, in the eighteenth, it was the Swiss writers and scholars themselves who actively intervened in the intellectual development of Europe. In his *Lettres sur les Anglais et les Français* the Bernese patrician, Beat Ludwig von Muralt, shortly before 1700 (and therefore long before Voltaire did a similar thing in his *Lettres philosophiques ou anglaises*) compared the two nations, England and France, their culture, mentality and literature and, terrible to say, he found the celebrated France under Louis XIV totally wanting. Muralt, the real discoverer of England, was thus chronologically the first among the innumerable continentals (Montesquieu, Voltaire, Rousseau, Rolli, Baretti, van Effen and others) for whom England became the Mecca of their pilgrimages. A generation later, Johann Jakob

Bodmer from Zürich, the famous translator of *Paradise Lost*, and also of *Hudibras* and of the *Dunciad*, became the head of a whole school of Anglophiles, the first true pre-Romanticist who made Zürich a fountainhead for the new trends to come. Let us stop for a moment to consider how very important the Milton-translation by this single Swiss intermediary Bodmer became for the whole further evolution of literature in eighteenth-century Germany—for after generations of drought and rationalism and dullest pedantry before and during the rather notorious age of Gottsched in Germany it was Bodmer who, with the help of Milton, at last brought back religious exaltation, lyricism, warmth, imagination and fantasy into literature, and thus announced the dawn of an as yet distant Romanticism. Bodmer's basic essays of 1740-41, *Ueber das Wunderbare in der Poesie* and *Ueber die poetischen Gemälde der Dichter*, signify more than a mere defeat of Gottsched and of the petrified French Neo-Classicism behind Gottsched in Germany, for this quarrel over Milton between Zürich and Leipzig was in truth also the last phase of the famous European Quarrel between the Ancients and the Moderns—and with Bodmer's victory the Moderns finally won their most promising battle. Bodmer was also among the first to emulate Addison's *Spectator* papers in his own *Discourse der Maler*, 1721 ff—and among the host of friends and compatriots who now set out to translate English authors systematically, let us mention Simon Grynaeus from Basel, who rendered into German both *Paradise Regained* and *Romeo and Juliet*, the French-Swiss Pierre Clément, the translator of Lillo's significant first bourgeois drama, *George Barnwell or the London Merchant*, and Louis Bridel from Lausanne, the emulator, in French, of *Ossian*. More than that: Bodmer's fellow-Züricher Salomon Gessner was not only a noted author, but also the owner of one of the oldest printing houses in the canton—and it was this Zürich firm that saw through press the first two German translations of Shakespeare's collected dramas, those by Wieland and by Eschenburg. Only the third translation of Shakespeare, the famous Schlegel version of 1797 ff, was then an all-German affair. It is usually stated that the new, fructifying influences from England entered the continent through three main gates: Amsterdam, Hamburg and Zürich. Amsterdam, because of men like Justus van Effen and a large Huguenot colony, and Hamburg, because of close commercial relations with English and Dutch ports, are logical clearing-houses for cultural matters also. But the task was much harder for landlocked, distant Zürich; and it took all the enthusiasm of Bodmer and his friends to make that city a center of anglophile activity, the mother of Pre-Romanticism, and to preserve a noble tradition of Anglo-Swiss cooperation which had been so mutually beneficent already in the sixteenth century.

This Swiss discovery of England was by no means the only feat of that kind. Later, about 1800, when after England Germany was to take over the leadership in European culture, it was again largely the Swiss who discovered and explained Germany to the rest of the Western World. By that is meant, of course, above all the fundamentally important book by Mme de Staël from Geneva, *De l'Allemagne*, the veritable Bible of European Romanticism. Yet even before her, another Genevan was a pioneer in a different Germanic field—namely in the unleashing of the so-called Nordic Renaissance. Scandinavian influences grew in intensity in this increasingly anti-French and anti-classical eighteenth century: Sir William Temple, the Whartons and Collins in England, and Gerstenberg and Klopstock in Germany had begun to dwell on the virile impact of Nordic culture, religion and literature —yet it was only with Paul Henri Mallet, a Genevan long residing in Copenhagen, that this long-dormant treasure was finally made known to Western European readers. I am referring not so much to his *Histoire du Danemark* of 1755, but to his *Monumenta* appended to this *Histoire* in which, to illustrate the points raised, he rendered into French old texts from the *Edda* about Scandinavian mythology, literature and martial customs. Others immediately translated Mallet, for example Bishop Percy in his *Northern Antiquities*, or profited by him, as did Gray in his runic odes, or as Herder did in the increasingly pro-Nordic orientation of his philosophy of life.

The same pro-Nordic bias, pro-Scandinavian, pro-English, pro-German, can be found in the essay by Mme de Staël, *De la littérature considérée dans ses rapports avec les institutions sociales*, and especially in her *De l'Allemagne* of 1813, which now informed all the later European romanticists—the Montis in Italy, the Hugos in France, the Lakists in England, indeed the Emersons in America—about the greatness of the new golden age of German literature, all the more so since ever so many of these romanticists had a better knowledge of French than of German, and therefore needed an intermediary, a translator, to tell them about Goethe, Schiller, Kant or Kleist. Another Swiss to share in this task of making Germany known to the general European intelligentsia was Mme de Staël's lover, Benjamin Constant from Lausanne. He elaborated on the new literary currents in a thoughtful essay *Réflexions sur le théâtre allemand* and by translating Schiller's *Wallenstein* into a French five-act tragedy which, however, is greatly inferior to Coleridge's English rendering of the same trilogy. Nor should we forget the immense international significance of Coppet, Mme de Staël's estate near Geneva, which, owing largely to the extended visits there of August Wilhelm Schlegel, became the European headquarters of Romanticism just as, four to five decades before, Ferney, Voltaire's estate near Geneva, had been the headquarters for European Enlightenment. Everybody who was anybody went to Italy during the Romantic Age and therefore found it convenient as well as highly profitable to stop at Mme de Staël's in Coppet and get the latest pronunciamentos about Romantic theory straight from its high-priest, A. W. Schlegel. The most recent study of the impact of Coppet upon the visiting English romanticists is by Walter Häusermann, professor of English at the University of Geneva, while, years before, Carlo Pellegrini, professor of French in Florence, analyzed the importance of Coppet from the viewpoint of Italian literature.

Later in the nineteenth century, Switzerland, a pioneer and an intermediary *par excellence*, helped to make a third discovery after England and Germany, namely that of Italy, more particularly of the greatness of the Italian Renaissance. At a time when Europe was oscillating between the anti-Italian tenor of the so-called Gothic novels and the pro-Italian enthusiasm of the leading romanticists, Swiss authors from Bodmer to beyond Burckhardt helped to tip the scales in favor of Italy and of an Italian literature which had only too long been suppressed by the prejudices of the disciples of French Neo-Classicism.

74

Though the Germans, as we have seen, knew of Dante as a great theologian and polemicist, they had no true appreciation of his even greater qualities as a poet until Bodmer, in 1763, wrote the first chiefly literary evaluation of his genius in an essay called *Ueber das dreyfache Gedicht Dantes*. Evil tongues sometimes maintain that Bodmer wrote this careful analysis of the *Divine Comedy* mainly to help out Klopstock who, ever since the first three cantons of his *Messias* had appeared in 1748, had been bogged down in the continuation of his religious epic and therefore could use a helping hint or two from Bodmer. However that may be, from this pioneering essay of Bodmer on, the German enthusiasm for Dante also began to grow in leaps and bounds, as is indicated by translators and critics of the type of Bachenschwanz, Jagemann, the Schlegels, Philalethes, Karl Witte and others. To show Mme de Staël's exuberantly pro-Italian activity we should mention her novel *Corinne*, a book almost as significant for the revival of Italy as her *De l'Allemagne* had been for the meteoric rise of the international appreciation of Germany. *Corinne*, to be sure, was a love-story, her reply to Benjamin Constant's *Adolphe* — yet the two lovers, against the background of a glorious Italy, at times seem more concerned with loving evaluations of the greatness of Italian culture, and ardent reappraisals of great *cinquecentisti* of the type of Torquato Tasso, than with their own amorous problems.

Third and possibly even more important among these pro-Italian Swiss was Jean-Charles-Léonard de Sismondi, also from Geneva, who became a veritable historian of the greatness of the Italian Renaissance in his *Histoire des républiques italiennes du moyen âge* and his *Histoire de la Renaissance de la liberté en Italie* — while his vast *Histoire de la littérature du Midi de l'Europe* of 1813, a significant early work in Comparative Literature, again attributed a leading role to Italian literature against the background of French, Provençal, Spanish and Portuguese letters. All this, it should be noted, happened during an age in which the Frenchman Lamartine insulted the whole of Italy by calling it the Land of the Dead, and was promptly challenged to a duel for this slur. After Sismondi came the Italian-Swiss Giovanni Orelli, the friend of Manzoni and of Foscolo, the translator into German of the latter's famous Wertherian novel *Le ultime lettere di Jacopo Ortiz* and author of the *Croni-chette d'Italia*. Yet probably the greatest of these Swiss Italophiles was Jakob Burckhardt from Basel, whose epoch-making *Die Kultur der Re-naissance in Italien* of 1860 is a classic even today, more than a century later—a cultural historian who in his study of the essence of the Renais-sance certainly believed, together with his fellow-professor at the Uni-versity of Basel, Friedrich Nietzsche, that history is made by gigantic men beyond good and evil, and not by the nameless masses. Burckhardt was followed by Conrad Ferdinand Meyer from Zürich, one of the two finest prose-writers of German Switzerland, a consummate artist who specialized in historical novels—quite a few among them again dealing with the Italian Renaissance, for instance *Die Hochzeit des Mönchs* of 1883 about the *trecento*, and *Die Versuchung des Pescara* about the *cinque-cento*.

These allusions to the high points in the intermediary role of Switzer-land in the eighteenth and early nineteenth centuries with regard to England, Germany and Italy (so masterfully presented by F. Ernst in his above-mentioned book) must break off here, for we cannot afford to include also the role of Switzerland as a shelter for refugees or an inspirer for foreign guests, as we had been doing in the case of the six-teenth century. Such a listing would include Montesquieu, a student of Swiss democracy, and Voltaire, the patriarch of Ferney, among the French; Wieland, Klopstock, Goethe, Zschokke, Kleist among the Germans; the historian Gibbon and Byron, author of *The Prisoner of Chillon*, among the English; indeed also Longfellow, author of *Hyperion*, and James Fenimore Cooper among the Americans—the latter a most grouchy visitor to Europe with admiration, it seems, for Switzerland alone. We could continue some of these investigations to include the last hundred years, as Albert Bettex from Zürich recently did with regard to Germany (*Spiegelungen der Schweiz in der deutschen Literatur seit* 1870) and we could say that Richard Wagner found refuge in Lucerne; that Friedrich Nietzsche taught in Basel and Adam Mickie-wicz in Lausanne; that during World War I Romain Rolland from France and René Schickele from Germany came to live in Switzerland; that the two greatest German poets of modern times, Rainer Maria

Rilke and Stefan George, both lived and died in Switzerland, or that James Joyce spent a significant period of his life in Zürich. Sometimes these foreign guests were political refugees like Mazzini, at times quite unwelcome because of their radicalism as, for instance, Lenin and Mussolini in their early manhood. Often they were friendly literary figures who even wrote about their new homeland as, for instance, Thomas Mann in his *Der Zauberberg*, or Ricarda Huch in her *Erinnerungen von Ludolf Ursleu dem Jüngeren*; indeed, at times they even became naturalized Swiss citizens, like Hermann Hesse. But all these new facts would not add to the basic impression of the intermediary role of Switzerland I have tried to convey—and if we all dream of a united Western World, perhaps patterned after this Swiss microcosm, in which there shall, some day, be tolerance and justice and goodwill, with a free, lively intercourse of all sorts of ideas in all sorts of languages, then we can perhaps, hopefully, agree with Victor Hugo's prophetic assertion that "La Suisse, dans l'histoire, aura le dernier mot!"

Scholars outside Germany have found it hard to accept the term "Baroque" for the literature between 1550 and 1650; instead, they have preferred to use the term "Late Renaissance" and thus to extend the validity of that word "Renaissance" over many dissimilar centuries and currents extending from Petrarch to Milton. It is the purpose of this article to underscore the immense differences that exist between the real Renaissance and that so-called "Late Renaissance", and to propose that, in lieu of that very misleading and inaccurate term, the considerably less unsatifactory word "Baroque" (if we emphasize form) or "Counter-Reformation" (if we emphasize thought) should be used. By thus underlining the very real differences between the early sixteenth and early seventeenth centuries, I do not mean to deny knowledge of the continuous evolution of human thought and productivity, nor do I wish to belittle the very real contributions the Baroque Age made to the scientific renaissance in Europe; I merely wish to contrast the two ages strongly enough to make it clear that the same word, Renaissance–Early and Late–should not obtain for both of them, because they are very different in their mentality.

The specialists in English literature particularly very frequently persist in ending their Renaissance with Bunyan's *Pilgrim's Progress* or in asserting that the Metaphysical Poets have no exact parallel on the European Continent. Against this belief I should like to present the Baroque Age as a definite reality, whose phenomena are apparent in all countries of Western Europe, in Spain, Germany, and France as well as in England.

---

[1]Paper read in the Philological Club at UNC in the fall of 1945 and published in the *Journal of English and Germanic Philology* XLVI, 1947, 132-43.

The term "Late Renaissance" is positively inaccurate and misleading for that period; nor does it seem possible to substitute the rather colorless designation "The Seventeenth Century" for it, because the year 1660 both in France and in England splits up that century into two utterly different parts. It is rare for literary historians to be at a loss to find a proper name for a certain literary period. Yet we cannot dismiss this question too lightly, and since we all know what the thing is, there is no reason why we should not find a good name for it, borrowing it from political and religious history — Counter-Reformation — if the term suggested by and borrowed from the Fine Arts — Baroque — does not suit us. Both terms are avowedly unsatisfactory; yet they are far superior to "Late Renaissance." In many respects the word "Baroque" resembles the word "Romanticism": it can serve as a useful general label, though it covers a multitude of aspects and is capable of an imposing number of definitions.

Theologians and historians are perfectly right when they, in their very terms Reformation and Counter-Reformation, indicate that the two periods are quite hostile towards each other, as different from one another as day and night. Literary historians should follow them and possibly create the word "Counter-Renaissance," for the events after 1550 were a counter-revolution indeed. It was a period when ecclesiastical and worldly rulers alike tried to undo the spirit of personal, intellectual, and religious freedom that had dawned over Europe and when poets no less than liberal leaders (Egmont), religious thinkers (Bruno), and bold scientists (Galileo) had to bear the brunt of an increasingly cruel intolerance. It was a last attempt by the powers that be to undo the Renaissance and the Reformation and to restore the impressive and oppressive greatness and unity which had been the Middle Ages.

A few facts and dates will make my point clear; they will explain that somewhere in the sixteenth century — at different times in different nations — a great divide was indeed reached. In referring to aspects of individual national literatures, I shall have to apologize to the specialists among readers who may find some remarks rather elementary; the value and the novelty (if any) of this brief outline lie in the fact that we shall notice that the same mental and literary phenomena can be traced in all the countries of Western Europe and that the baroque mentality is not merely a chimera. When exactly was the exuberant and universal spirit of the Renaissance broken and when did the orthodoxy and the bigotry of the Church (supported by the increasing absolutism of the monarchs) reassert themselves and endeavor to bring man back under the yoke of supreme authority?

Italy, the first to start the Renaissance, was also the first to witness the end of that proud period and to go down in subjection and humiliation—at a time indeed when other nations were still in the midst of their Renaissance effusiveness. Many dates can be suggested to designate the moment when the Italian day changed into night: 1525, the date of the battle of Pavia, not so important because it marked the end of the French political aspirations on the peninsula, but deeply significant because from that year on the power of Spanish troops and Spanish intolerance was supreme in Italy for almost two hundred years; or 1527, the date of the Sack of Rome by the German-Spanish troops of Charles V, a misdeed which in many ways symbolizes the way the invasions of foreign barbarians into the "giardino dell' Europa" put an end to the greatness that had been the Italian Renaissance; or 1530, the date of the fall of Florence, marking the end of the last Italian city republic, and its renewed subjection to the increasing absolutism of the Medicis. Religious rather than political events marking the end of the Italian Renaissance all occur a few years later and are utterly alien to the preceding age of Lodovico Ariosto and Leonardo da Vinci: the introduction of the Spanish Inquisition, the founding of the order of the Jesuits, the beginning of the Church Council of Trent, in which the Catholic Church made efficient plans for a counteroffensive against Protestantism, and, finally, the establishment of the *Index librorum prohibitorum*. The result of all this is well known: a complete Italian blackout, a period of two hundred years which produced only three great names: Tasso, Bruno, and Galileo, before Vico, Parini and Alfieri in the eighteenth century picked up the threads again.

If Italy was the leader in the European Renaissance, Spain surely was the literary leader during the Age of the Counter-Reformation—so very much so that the terms for her Golden Century and for the Counter-

Reformation or Baroque Age are quite interchangeable. That *Siglo de Oro* is usually said to have lasted from 1547, the date of Cervantes' birth, till 1635, the date of Lope's death. Renaissance exuberance in Spain, though clearly mainfest during her great age of transatlantic discoveries, had never turned so much against Church or King as in other countries; at Villalar in 1521 Charles V had quickly asserted his royal superiority against rebellious communities, and the few *erasmistas* like Juan de Valdés, Alfonso de Valdés, and Luis Vives who followed Erasmus of Rotterdam in a moderate criticism of Catholicism were the exception rather than the rule. The transition from the freedom of the Renaissance to the absolute submissiveness of the Baroque was hence not so great in Spain as elsewhere. If we look for convenient dates to mark the change, we may choose 1556, when the austere Philip II succeeded his father to the throne of Spain; or 1563, the end of the Church Council of Trent, when the necessary steps against Protestantism had been decided upon; or 1568, when Spain indicated through her fanatical zeal in the Netherlands that she marched at the head of the great Catholic host of the Counter-Reformation.

For France the great divide was surely reached in 1572, the date of the St. Bartholomew's Massacre. The twenty-five years before that date witnessed the peak of the French Renaissance, the *Pléiade* of Ronsard and du Bellay and, even earlier than that, the quite symbolical marriage of Henry II to Catherine of Medici, mother of the three succeeding French kings; but what followed after 1572 was religious hatred, a triangular civil war, and the powerful literature of du Bartas and d'Aubigné.

If we look for an equally decisive turning point in English history and literature, when the tremendous vitality and optimism of the Renaissance gave way to religious strife, to a new turmoil of souls and to ever stronger attempts to increase the absolutism of worldly princes and religious leaders alike, we may best choose the year 1603, the end of the Age of Elizabeth, when the accession of the Stuarts to the throne inaugurated almost ninety years of internal disorder.[2]

[2]There are German critics who insist that the Renaissance-Baroque cleavage runs through the very midst of Shakespeare's literary activity, with the bulk of the comedies belonging

As to Germany: it is a moot question whether the country that gave birth to the Reformation ever really experienced an aesthetic Renaissance in the Italo-French sense of that word;[3] but whether it did or not, the year 1618, *i.e.* the outbreak of the Thirty Years' War, certainly marked the end of the era of bourgeois emancipation and of an earthy, good-natured joy of living, and the beginning of a new age of religious fanaticism and princely absolutism.

Space permits me to point to only two types of literature which characterize the Age of the Counter-Reformation very well and about which I should like to say a few words in order to show how alien they are to the spirit of Lorenzo Valla's or Castiglione's Renaissance: the new upsurge of religious poetry (especially lyric poetry) and the martyr-plays.

Baroque literature is, above all, characterized by the sudden and violent clash between the pagan sensualism of the Renaissance on the one hand, and the newly asserted spiritualism, asceticism, and fanaticism of the Age of the Counter-Reformation on the other hand. This resulted in tragic conflicts in the souls of men and an ugly, at times cacophonic, discrepancy in the content as well as in the style of their literature. Only the Age of Classicism after 1660 could at long last establish a synthesis between these two conflicting trends; but during the baroque period proper men were constantly torn between exalted spiritualism and crude sensualism, between Christ and Venus, between Heaven and Hell. Some poets remained altogether sensual, like Carew and Suckling in England, under whose pen the healthy paganism of the Renaissance was transformed into the elegant filth and obscenity typical of the Stuart court; other poets became completely religious and spiritual,

to the optimistic period before 1600 and the bulk of tragedies (*Hamlet*, *Macbeth*) belonging to the pessimistic, Baroque period after 1600. Cf. Max Deutschbein: "Shakespeare und die Renaissance" (*Neuere Sprachen*, 1916) and *Shakespeare's Macbeth als Drama des Barock* (Leipzig, 1936); and Werner Weisbach: "Eine Shakespeare-Reform aus dem Geiste des Barock" (*Literarisches Echo*, 1924). Against that viewpoint cf. especially: Eduard Eckhardt: "Gehört Shakespeare zur Renaissance oder zum Barock?" (*Festschrift Friedrich Kluge zum 70. Geburtstage*, Tübingen, 1926).

[3]Cf. my article "Gibt es eine deutsche Renaissance?" *Mélanges offerts à H. Chamard*, Paris, 1951.

like Herbert and Milton,[4] men who were determined to stem the tide of ungodliness and to restore the power of religion on earth.

Many, however—and they are the most interesting poets for our purpose—represented the dual aspects of the Baroque Age in their own persons and works. They were men never at peace with themselves, unable to establish any harmony between the spirit and the flesh—like John Donne, who was sensual to the point of crudity, yet Dean of St. Paul's; like Robert Herrick, who wrote some of the most gracefully epicurean Renaissance verses, yet was a clergyman by profession and duly composed a considerable number of religious poems against the sins and temptations of this world; or like Richard Crashaw, a Catholic strongly influenced by the Italian and Spanish baroque authors, whose ardent mysticism, as was so often the case, was permeated with a strong dose of eroticism. The same haplessly split personalities we see in other literatures: the rather unconvincing *Oeuvres chrétiennes* by Philippe Desportes contrast shrilly with the voluptuous tone of all the other poems by this belated French Petrarchist—and in Germany Martin Opitz' translation of the *Songs of Songs* provides a typical example of the literature of that Janus-faced period in which glittering obscenities and fervent religious protestations were completely and bombastically intermingled. Mario Praz was quite right when he pointed out that Maria Magdalena was the favorite heroine of these baroque authors, for she was a saint *and* a harlot, a pagan *and* a Christian, a Venus in sackcloth, the perfect symbol of the spirit of the Renaissance broken and fettered by the new age of the religious Counter-Renaissance.[5]

[4]Though there is no doubt that the poet of *Paradise Lost* is one of the finest incarnations of the baroque mentality, it should be noted, too, that in matters of style he, the thoroughly trained scholar of ancient and modern literatures, is quite classical. Nor does the anti-royal rebelliousness of his Puritan faith agree with the usual submissiveness of the fawning baroque court-poets.

[5]Mario Praz: *Secentismo e Marinismo in Inghilterra: John Donne - Richard Crashaw*. Firenze, 1925, p. 147: "Nelle arti figurative come in letteratura, il motivo vien ripetuto inestancabilmente: nella bella peccatrice, effigiata nel fiore della giovinezza, che si spoglia delle pompe mondane e, discinta e vestita di ruvidi panni, versa l'argenteo fiume delle sue lacrime sui piedi del Redentore, e li rasciuga con l'aureo fiume delle sue chiome, l'epoca doveva riconoscersi come in uno specchio.... A quell' età erotica la grande amorosa penitente—Venere in cilicio—indicava la via della redenzione, la possibilità della gloria eterna."

Let it be emphasized, however, that not all men were torn by such conflicts and that quite a few poets in that age of vigorous religious reassertion sang loftily and beautifully in tones unimpeded by the temptations and the sinfulness of men—for instance, the great Spanish mystics of the second half of the sixteenth century, poets like Luis de León or San Juan de la Cruz, and in the Germany of the Thirty Years' War, powerful Protestant hymn-writers like Paul Gerhardt, Paul Fleming and Johannes Rist, whose impressive songs to this day fill the hymn-books of Germany, indeed even of England and America. Of course, it can be argued that Luther had already written church-hymns; but even a rapid comparison of the optimistic and vigorous "Ein' feste Burg ist unser Gott" with the songs of Gerhardt indicates clearly that the Germany of the seventeenth century was pessimistic, fearful, and desperate in groping its way back to God.[6] The same holds true for the other religious lyricists of that age: Protestants like Andreas Gryphius, Catholics like Friedrich von Spee, mystics like Angelus Silesius.

The impact of the newly-born religious fervor also destroyed the relatively peaceful and indifferent co-existence that had begun to prevail among the Christian and the pagan gods. In the great Portuguese national epic of Os Lusiadas it is quite touching to observe the blissful harmony that still existed between Christian and pagan mythology, and to hear prayers addressed to God as well as to Zeus, to watch the miraculous interventions of Saint Mary as well as of Venus, or to dread the sinister machinations of a Christian devil as well as of a pagan Bacchus. But that naive harmony of Camoens is destroyed as soon as the impact of the Counter-Reformation becomes really felt, and the protagonists will henceforth again be poles apart, as in Milton's Paradise Lost, when the ones are all good and the others are all bad. Renaissance and Baroque thus more and more seem like thesis and antithesis: the one is all pagan, the other all Christian in its mentality—and only

[6]It is a moot question just how great and how quick was the influence of Copernicus upon the generations after him, but there can be no doubt that this De revolutionibus orbium caelestium (published in 1543) must have enlightened his readers about the smallness, the insignificance, and the impotence of the human race and of this world of ours and must hence have added to their utter pessimism, bewilderment, and despair.

Classicism can then at last find the synthesis, in Racine's *Andromaque* of 1667, or in Goethe's *Iphigenie* 120 years later, when modern Christianity and Greek paganism at long last are blended into one organic and harmonious masterpiece. Such a tolerant and broadminded solution would have been unimaginable for the baroque poets, for in their religious crisis they could think only of sin and damnation and of the tragically punished presumptuousness of gods (as in Joost van den Vondel's *Lucifer*) and of men (as in Giovanbattista Andreini's *Adamo*). There was no synthesis, no peace and harmony possible for them.

The great vogue of martyr-plays that swept over Europe early in the seventeenth century likewise characterizes well the mentality of the Baroque Age, with its emphasis on pessimism, on the vanity of all human endeavors, on the frightfulness of hell-fire, and with its belief that life is only a dream (cf. Calderón's *La vida es sueño*) or, worse, a nightmare. Everything had become problematical in life; man was no longer a gigantic, optimistic demi-god, but a reed in the wind, a falling leaf, a thin cloud of smoke, a dwindling snow-flake unable to face an omnipotent and horribly wrathful Jehovah. Nothing could save him except *constantia* — perseverance, an unflinching faith in spite of all fears, temptations, sufferings. Hence now the new love of martyr-plays, depicting heroes and heroines who were willing to forego everything in life and who calmly endured the worst cruelties and tortures for the sake of the slim chance of gaining the Kingdom of Heaven. It is needless to add that the Jesuit dramas, powerful influences working all over Europe for the cause of the Counter-Reformation, achieved an impressive greatness also in this field of martyr-tragedies.

As secular examples of that type of literature we can mention Vondel's *De Maagden* in Holland, Philip Massinger's *The Virgin Martyr* in England, or Calderón's *El principe constante* in Spain. Even more interesting is *El mágico prodigioso*, also by Calderón, for this Spanish treatment of a Faustian theme does not end, as in Goethe later, with a glorification of man's intellectual ambitions; instead, it is a typically Catholic spectacle with a grand finale about the mercifulness of divine grace and the eagerness of the formerly wicked magician, Cipriano, to suffer tortures and death with his Christian lady-love, Justina, for the greater glory of the Christian God. And in Germany, of course, it was Andreas Gryphius who was the most prolific author of martyr-plays and the greatest poet during a relatively barren century.

France, too, participated in this upsurge of religious exaltation – not only her Huguenots, but also her Catholics, who from St. François de Sales on, through Bourdaloue and Bossuet, experienced a real *renaissance catholique*, a Catholic regeneration which in many ways found its finest expression in the Jansenists of Port-Royal. This religious fervor resulted in a considerable number of religious epics of the type of Desmarest de Saint-Sorlin's *Clovis* and of Antoine Godeau's *Saint Paul*, until Boileau protested against their over-emphasis of "le merveilleux chrétien"; it resulted also in a number of martyr-tragedies, for which Garnier's *Les Juifves* had already provided the proper atmosphere. We need not go into Corneille's *Polyeucte*, the best-known French representative of this type; instead, I want to point out a second martyr-play by the same author, who in many respects was much more baroque than classical: his *Théodore* of 1646 – a play which in some respects resembles Massinger's *Virgin Martyr* and which caused quite an animated controversy, because Corneille had dared to show how the staunch Christian heroine was thrown to the soldiers, something the increasingly classical French audience would not stand for. Another very interesting martyr-drama is Rotrou's *Saint Genest*: it shows a play within a play and demonstrates well the miracle of sudden Christian inspiration and divine grace, for a pagan actor who is supposed to play the role of a Christian martyr now suddenly, on the stage, becomes a Christian himself, and his gruesome end, of a sudden, becomes truth and reality, rather than mere make-believe.

These, then, are two aspects of Western European literature around 1600 which may induce us to choose the term "Counter-Reformation" rather than "Late Renaissance" for the literature of this period. If we do so, however, we must take the word Counter-Reformation in the widest possible sense. It applies not only to the Catholics, to the decisions of the Church Council of Trent which were put into practice by

Philip II in Spain and the Netherlands, by the Hapsburgs in Austria, by Mary Tudor in England and by the queen-mother Catherine of Medici and the Guise brothers in France; it applies also to the Protestants, who likewise became more fanatical and bigoted as time went on. Luther's morning call for a new freedom in 1517 was short-lived indeed; as early as 1525, fearful of the avalanche he himself had started, he repudiated that freedom when he turned against the rebellious peasants of Germany who in his name had risen against their masters. After Luther's death the German Protestants in their bigotry did not seem one whit better than the Catholics from whom they had seceded; and in Geneva, too, Calvin certainly was not preaching freedom the way the Renaissance had understood it. The Puritans in England and America, the Huguenots and Jansenists in France, the Jesuits in Spain, Italy, and Austria, the Lutherans in Germany were all really birds of a feather, and their rigidity of attitude could be broken only after the Thirty Years' War had shown the criminal absurdity of religious intolerance, and after the Age of Rationalism, from Descartes on, began to nullify the efforts of the religious zealots to lead the world back into a new medieval bondage. We can point, of course, to exceptions, to figures of light during this period of darkness: to Montaigne in France, Bruno in Italy, Bacon in England and, above all, to one of the most inspiring battlers for human freedom, Roger Williams in Rhode Island — but these are only exceptions that prove the rule; their existence in no way contradicts what we have said about the decades that lie between Loyola and Cromwell.

The word "Baroque," to whose definition and applicability we now turn, originated among Spanish-Portuguese jewelers and it was meant to designate stones that were irregular, uncouth, not polished, not perfect. Historians of art, especially Wölfflin in Zürich,[7] adopted it to designate the period that lay between the Renaissance of the sixteenth and the Rococo of the eighteenth century, for instance the art of Bernini, or the architecture of Salzburg and Prague. In a significant essay pub-

[7]Heinrich Wölfflin: *Renaissance und Barock*. München, 1888.

lished in 1916 Fritz Strich[8] was the first to apply that term to literature, too, to the entire seventeenth century in Germany, where it is now unchallenged and definitely established. Other countries were more reluctant to follow, but Benedetto Croce[9] wrote an interesting essay on the Italian Baroque, and Pfandl[10] in his great history of the *Siglo de Oro* in Spain even distinguishes between the Age of the Counter-Reformation (up to the death of Philip II) and the Baroque Literature of the entire seventeenth century, from Philip III to the death of the last Spanish Hapsburg ruler, Charles II. In France the term Baroque has sometimes been used to designate the literature of the reigns of Henry IV and Louis XIII, and in English literature many publications have tried to apply it to the strife-torn period of Cavaliers and Puritans.[11]

In art as well as in literature, Baroque may be said to be the degeneration of the beauty and simplicity that had been the Renaissance. For the religious poets and artists the world had lost its harmony and its serene optimism; hence now discrepancies, conflicts, tensions, and crisis, which were at once reflected in the works of the new age. Renaissance art had been essentially static in its self-assured calm; baroque art, however, became dynamic, problem-ridden, torn by passions and fears. Simple words were no longer sufficient for the baroque poet; hence the endless enumerations of nouns and glittering adjectives; hence also the incessant search for new metaphors, antitheses and hyperboles — yet all of these agglomerations were really utterly inadequate to communicate the

[8]Fritz Strich: "Der lyrische Stil des 17. Jahrhunderts." *Abhandlungen zur deutschen Literaturgeschichte, Franz Muncker dargebracht.* München, 1916.

[9]Benedetto Croce: *Der Begriff des Barock. Die Gegenreformation. Zwei Essays.* Zürich, 1925. Cf. also his *Storia della Età Barocca in Italia.* Bari, 1929.

[10]Ludwig Pfandl: *Geschichte der spanischen Nationalliteratur in ihrer Blütezeit.* Freiburg, 1929. Quite typical of the different attitude of other literary historians, however, are Hurtado, Serna and Palencia in their *Historia de la Literatura española* (Madrid, 1940) and Ernest Mérimée in his *Précis d'Histoire de la Littérature espagnole* (Paris, 1922). The former discuss the entire sixteenth and seventeeeth centuries under the general heading of "la literatura castellana durante la Casa de Austria"; the latter subdivides the field into " La Renaissance" (De Juan II à Carlos V) and "Le Siècle d'Or" (Du second tiers de XVIe siècle à la mort de Calderón).

[11]Fritz Pützer: *Prediger des englischen Barock, stilistisch untersucht.* Bonn, 1929. W. F. Schirmer: "Die geistesgeschichtlichen Grundlagen der englischen Barockliteratur." *Germanisch-Romanische Monatsschrift,* 1931.

great emotion the poet wanted to express. Painters, poets, and architects alike worked with shrill colors and double and triple adornments, as though nothing less would do to help them assert themselves in the midst of this tragically ephemeral world of ours.

Baroque poets of an entirely different type joined the religious authors in their effort to create *fortissimo* effects: the erotic poets of the post-Renaissance period, who likewise forsook simplicity of language in favor of bombast and ponderousness. These poets, whether they be sweetish Petrarchists or naturalistic anti-Petrarchists, now vied with each other in making poetry a purely intellectual game full of exotic phraseology, tricky constructions, unexpected antitheses, gushing metaphors, daring somersaults—all of them calculated to astound rival poets and lady-loves alike. Petrarch's own sonnets had shown the germs of this degeneration; almost two centuries after him Italian poets like Serafino, Cariteo, and Tansillo. and neo-Latin poets beyond the Alps like Eobanus Hessus and Johannes Secundus accelerated that trend, and anti-Petrarchists of the type of Berni joined them with exaggerated buffoonery. And thus we see indeed the worshippers of Christ on the one side, and the worshippers of Venus on the other side, joining hands in their turgid bulkiness and repetitiousness of style. Mock-heroic epics like Tassoni's *La secchia rapita* and Christian epics like du Bartas' *Semaine*, the ribald poems of Sir John Suckling and the pious verses of Mrs. Ann Bradstreet, the stern martyr-tragedies of Gryphius and the blood-curdling displays of lust, perversity, and Senecan horror of Lohenstein: they all belong together as works of the same period of complete mental instability and of stylistic extravagance.

Though the Germans may call their seventeenth-century literature "Baroque" and may try to extend that name to other European literatures as well, other nations have often preferred other names for these aberrations around 1600—aberrations, by the way, which then either died of their own excesses or which were liquidated by the somewhat strait-laced sanity of Boileau's Classicism after 1660. In Italy, these mannerisms and *concetti* of the *secento* reached their apex in the glittering voluptuousness and the bombastic exaggerations contained in Marino's epic *Adone*; hence they are aften called *secentismo* or Marinism. In Spain, though appearing quite strongly already in 1529 in the *Libro aureo del emperador Marco Aurelio (Relox de Principes)* by Antonio de Guevara, they reached their climax in Góngora's lyrical poetry and are hence called Gongorism—though Mérimée suggests two other terms: *conceptisme* and *cultisme—conceptisme*, the graver of the two offenses, being the malady of becoming too subtle and over-sophisticated in thought, whereas *cultisme* (which he declares to be identical with Gongorism) applied only to style and was merely a consequence of the primary disease, *conceptisme*. The first wave of the same phenomenon in England was called Euphuism, after John Lyly's *Euphues* of 1580, while the poets of the second wave, early in the seventeenth century, are mostly called Metaphysical Poets, indulging in what Professor Babbitt at Harvard used to designate as "intellectual romanticism." And in France, finally, poets like Voiture and the ladies of the Hôtel de Rambouillet, who had chosen Marino as their great literary model, are commonly said to belong to the school of *Préciosité*, indulging in a literary vice which the sober Molière later satirized in *Les précieuses ridicules*.

One important observation should be made, however, though I may be slightly prejudiced in making it: namely that all the bad things that may be said and have been said against baroque literature are really justified only in the case of the worldly poets and not of the religious poets—and, if we want to be specific among the latter, the reproaches are justified only in the case of most Catholic authors, and not of the Protestant authors. For the Catholics, never having broken away from Rome and never having burnt their bridges as completely behind them as the Protestants had, were not seized half as grippingly and as fearfully by the impact of the Counter-Reformation, and their ugliness of style is hence not justifiable on the grounds of mental torture. The Protestants, on the other hand, had no elaborate Catholic hierarchy to guide them, no firmly established dogma to reassure them; alone and unaided, they had to face the new wave of orthodoxy which thundered against their former spiritual and physical emancipation and against the proud individualism of yesterday; and their souls, tormented by unceasing visions of hell-fire and damnation imposed upon men by a cruel Jehovah who could only kill and punish, had to struggle along as best they could in this miserable valley of tears. Hence the outcries, the despair, the endless protestations in their literature; hence the awkward, cumbersome, overladen, and cacophonous qualities of their style —for these men wrote under a pressure almost too great to be borne. The frightful visions contained in d'Aubigné's *Tragiques* in France, the ponderous mysticism of Jakob Boehme in Germany, the heavy, involved style of John Donne's *Sermons* in England and of Richard, Increase, and Cotton Mather in America all have to be read and understood against such a background. If we study literature for the sake of the aesthetic pleasure we may derive from it, we must never turn to the Baroque Age, for it will bitterly disappoint us, if not disgust us; but if we study literature because we want to know the souls, the problems, the conflicts, the hopes and sufferings of men in a given age, then baroque literature indeed opens up for investigation a tragically rich field, whose works in the end cannot but move us deeply. For even if they do bring in Senecan horrors and show the worst possible tortures on the stage, as for instance in Gryphius' tragedies, we know that it is all done *ad majorem gloriam Dei*, that Gryphius does not show lust and murder in order to tickle our senses, but merely in order the more to affirm and to glorify man's imperative need to turn to God in all things.

Compared with this meaningful literature of the Protestant authors, the baroque works of some Catholic poets and of the entire clan of erotic poets of all creeds and all nations appear unimportant and empty indeed, for as very much belated and insincere Petrarchists, or as emphatic anti-Petrarchists, they did nothing but grind over and over again twice-ground corn, filling their laboriously manufactured sonnets—not with new and genuine thoughts, far from it—but with new metaphors, antitheses, and other acrobatics. The Desportes and Voitures in France, the Chiabrinis and Marinos in Italy, the Carews and Rochesters in England, the Lohensteins and Hofmannswaldaus in Germany did not add very much to the world's literature; with most of them the enviably healthy sensualism of the Renaissance gradually turned into pornography, and the lucid simplicity of style into stilted and bloated artificiality. The wave of the Counter-Reformation touched them only in so far as it made them convinced of the ultimate damnation of all sinners—and this being so, they were resolved to empty their cup of pleasure to the very dregs, singing their *Carpe diem* gracefully and beautifully as did Robert Herrick, or filthily as did Suckling. Their works deserve most of the bad things modern students of literature like to say about the Baroque Age; but the religious, the Protestant poets, in my opinion, ought to be excepted from the general condemnation, for there is gold in them, no matter how many thick layers we have to dig through in order to reach it.

In conclusion I should like to emphasize one last point about baroque literature. It is not only a somewhat elemental type of literature, unwieldly in form and in thought; it is also the last great bulwark against the classical principles of literature which the Italians and especially the French gradually tried to impose upon Western Europe. Pseudo-classical rules had first been formulated in Italy; we usually refer to Trissino's *Sofonisba* of 1515 as the first pseudo-classical tragedy, to Ariosto's various plays as the first pseudo-classical comedies, to Cardinal Bembo as the first pseudo-classical lyricist, and to Tasso's reworked *Gerusalemme conquistata* as the first pseudo-classical epic. But the Italians did not go beyond these earliest beginnings, perhaps because they were incapable of the discipline and the pathos of real Classicism. The French, therefore, picked up the thread where the Italians had left off, with Jodelle, Garnier, and Jean de la Taille in the second half of the sixteenth century, and with Malherbe, Mairet, and Corneille continuing these efforts in the first half of the seventeenth century, until at last they were perfected into the sublime form of the French Classicism of 1660.

But other European countries were more than reluctant to follow the French example, for neither the exuberance of the Renaissance nor the intense conflicts of the Counter-Reformation lent themselves particularly well to being forced into the strait-jacket of pseudo-classical rules. Generalizing rather broadly we may perhaps say that England accepted Pseudo-Classicism about half-way, though many medieval and romantic traditions still remained at work in her literature and though she was soon intent on safeguarding these English liberties and irregularities against the encroachments of Pseudo-Classicism emanating from France. Nevertheless, we can notice a straight line of half-willingly classicizing authors extending from Norton and Sackville's *Gorboduc* through Ben Jonson and Dryden to Addison's *Cato*—though it should not be too hard to prove that muddling Dryden and Addison were just about as anti-classical as they were pro-classical.[12]

Spain and Germany offered even stronger resistance, for they were rich in great native, utterly unclassical, traditions which they were loath to surrender. The two greatest forms of literature emanating from the Golden Age of Spanish literature, the irregular *comedia* and the *novela*—especially the picaresque novel—were completely unclassical; a mere glance at Guillén de Castro's *Mocedades del Cid* and at Corneille's *Cid* shows us the deep abyss that separated the two concepts and the two nations. In fact we can say that of all Spaniards only Cervantes just once dabbled in Pseudo-Classicism when in 1585 he wrote the war-filled tragedy *La Numancia*. It is very interesting to read Lope de Vega's versified treatise on the *Arte nuevo de hacer comedias* of 1609, for in this essay on the new manner of writing dramas he says that he knows perfectly well what the new Aristotelian rules of writing are, but that he locks up the models of Antiquity under six keys, because the Spanish public does not like them, and that hence he will always continue to write his own *comedias* in the approved and irregular Spanish fashion.[13]

The same reluctance is to be noticed in Germany: around 1620, to be sure, Martin Opitz was the first to introduce pseudo-classical rules and to insist on the use of the French Alexandrine meter—and German dramatic authors like Gryphius and Lohenstein followed his directives; but in spite of Alexandrine meter, stilted dignity, catharsis, their pseudo-classical tragedies were unsatisfactory compromises, full of naturalism,

---

[12]It is quite a debatable question whether English baroque literature did not last considerably beyond 1660—as the pompousness of scenes, the pathos of action, or the flourishing of the opera would indicate in the age of Dryden, Otway, and Lee. Supporters of this assertion will maintain that English Neo-Classicism did not begin to prevail until the age of Pope.
[13]Y cuando he de escribir una comedia
encierro los preceptos con seis llaves;
saco a Terencio y Plauto de mi estudio
para que voces no me den...

Senecan blood and thunder, ghosts, and chorus, just as the English plays, too, had been, before the Puritans closed the theatres in 1642.

In other fields of literary activity, too, we see the same unwillingness or inability of the baroque authors to conform to the rules set up by Scaliger and Castelvetro, and it took the weighty impact of the great French Classical Age of Racine, Molière, and Boileau after 1660 to persuade the other European nations, decades later, early in the eighteenth century, to shed their baroque traditions and at last half-heartedly to accept the French teachings: Pope in England, Gottsched in Germany, Luzán in Spain, Goldoni in Italy.

The struggle of the last baroque authors was particularly pathetic in France: the *préciosité* of Voiture, Hardy's love of the Spanish *comedia* and Larrivey's of the Italian *commedia dell' arte*, the exuberant fantasy of Cyrano de Bergerac, the grotesque parodies and travesties by Scarron, the imitations of the earthy picaresque novels by Furetière and Sorel, the pastoral novels and dramas that spread in the wake of Sannazaro, Montemayor, Tasso, and d'Urfé, and finally the hybrid tragi-comedies that flourished in France throughout the reign of Louis XIII were all written by the last representatives of unfettered men, good, bad, or indifferent, who wrote as they pleased. Step by step they were crushed by Malherbe, by Richelieu's foundation of the *Académie Française*, by Mairet's *Sophonisbe* of 1634 and Corneille's *Cid* of 1636 (the first two really classical French tragedies), and they were overwhelmed even more by the publication of Descartes' treatises and by the failure of the Fronde (two events which had a profound influence upon literature, too), by the coming-of-age of Louis XIV in 1660 and, finally, by the publication of Boileau's *Art poétique* in 1674. That marked the end of the Baroque Age not only in France, but in Europe — for though Milton Lohenstein and Calderón still lived beyond that date, the days of their lives and of their literary beliefs were definitely numbered.

These, briefly, are some of the problems encountered in Western Europe between 1550 and 1650. I hope I have succeeded in my main purpose, which was to show that there is a well-nigh unbridgeable abyss between the Renaissance and the baroque Counter-Reformation — between Ariosto's

94

epicurean *Orlando Furioso* and Tasso's inhibited *Gerusalemme liberata*, between Rabelais' "Abbaye de Thélème" and Pascal's Jansenism, between Marlowe's *Faustus* and Bunyan's *Pilgrim's Progress*, between Ulrich von Hutten's joyous exclamation "Es ist eine Lust zu leben!" and Gryphius' gloomy and despairing *Vanitas, vanitatum vanitas* — and that these two utterly different periods in man's history should hence not be designated by the same confusing name of Renaissance, Early Renaissance for the former and Late Renaissance for the latter. But I am afraid it is still very much open to further discussion whether or not Counter-Reformation or Baroque is the generally acceptable better name. Personally I am in favor of the word "Baroque," for it is certainly a better and much more inclusive term than Marinism, Gongorism, Euphuism, Metaphysical Poetry, or whatever other words have been suggested instead.

IX. GERMAN BAROQUE TRAGEDY IN THE PERSPECTIVE
OF GREEK AND FRENCH CLASSICAL DRAMA[1]

The characteristics of the German baroque tragedy and the evolution from Gryphius to Lohenstein are sufficiently well know not to require recapitulation. To compare the quality, themes and technique of these two Germans with those of the golden ages of Greece before them, and of France shortly after them, is perhaps not quite as pointless as it may seem at first sight; for such an attempt, indirectly reflecting the whole national and social background of the Greek, German and French dramatists in question, transcends comparative *Literaturgeschichte* by giving important insights into comparative *Kulturgeschichte*.

In approaching our task, we naturally disregard the absurd praise heaped upon Lohenstein by Gryphius' son Christian ("Du hast dem Sophokles schon längst den Preis genommen / Und Aeschylus beseufzt, was er durch dich verlor"); instead, we can start by stating that, in many respects, Aeschylus is to Euripides as Gryphius is to Lohenstein.

Historically, there exists a great similarity between Greece at the time of the Peloponnesian War and the Germany of the Thirty Years' War. Both nations, after previous power, unity and greatness, were at that moment in a state of decay. Still worse, they hastened their decline by fighting suicidal civil wars. The intellectual and the religious unity of the two countries was broken. The rationalistic new generation no longer believed in the gods of Homer and Hesiod, or in the Christian God of the Middle Ages. Tradition and piety were belittled by the sceptics, the sophists, the libertines (see Thucydides II.53 and III.82);

---

[1]An amalgamation of two articles, "From Ethos to Pathos: The Development from Gryphius to Lohenstein" (*Germanic Review*, X, 1935, 223-36) and "German'and French Dramatic Topics of the Seventeenth Century" (*Studies in Philology*, XXXIV, 1937, 509-32) which had originally grown out of a talk given in Cincinnati in 1935.

neither the supreme power of Religion nor that of the State was strong enough to withstand the iconoclastic attitudes of a new age. In vain there arose valiant defenders of the old ideals who fought ardently for a return to the faith and patriotism of their forefathers. Neither the vigorous odes of Pindar, nor the German patriotism of Moscherosch and Logau, nor the religious ardor of Gryphius and Gerhardt could check the wavering of minds and the complete victory of Reason over Orthodoxy.

In the field of the tragedy, Aeschylus (our Gryphius), a gallant warrior in the Persian battles, was still a staunch defender of conservative, ethical ideals. His was an effort to justify the ways of the gods; again and again he expressed an unswerving faith in their justice. His tragedies, addressed to a young and increasingly emancipated generation, taught them ideals as lofty as those of Hesiod and Pindar. He extolled ancient times, exalting the mythological history of his forefathers, creating titanic personages, holding up their virtues and their piety as a brilliant example, and their evil passions as a warning to his contemporaries. The fate of Prometheus, who boasts of his emancipation and arrogantly demands equality between gods and men, is highly typical of the attitude of Aeschylus. It is a real condemnation of the sophists, and of the ridiculous new theories of means to control this world, for even new schools and new sciences will have to submit to the Olympians. Sophocles, though not less religious, already shows the beginnings of a reaction against Aeschylus' emphatic theodicy. For him and for the generation of Pericles, the gods are mysterious, unapproachable, often incomprehensible in their apparent cruelties (*Oedipus*). Nevertheless, the laws of religion and of piety are more important than the laws of man and of reason (*Antigone*); hence Sophocles' similarly strong opposition to the sophists. Then came Euripides (our Lohenstein), a real representative of the new age of emancipation. His dramas were no longer a defense of religion; on the contrary, they were an attack upon it. Aeschylus and Gryphius had always chosen some inspiring plot, driving home some great ethical truths (*Oresteia; Katharina von Georgien*). Sophocles had preserved the high ideals of his predecessor, but had rendered his dramas more human by showing real characters, men and women who do not merely serve as exemplifications of these truths, but already have a psyche of their own. Euripides and Lohenstein go farther in that direction; their heroes become unbridled, passionate, free from all moral and religious restrictions (*Medea; Ibrahim Sultan, Agrippina*). Bound to observe the traditional topics of the theatre and to rewrite what others before him had already treated, Euripides sheds new light upon these legends and, by his new rationalism and realism in *Electra* and *Orestes*, he challenges the versions of Aeschylus and Sophocles. The plays of Aeschylus, so lyrical on account of the preponderance of the chorus over the two actors, often tended, like those of Gryphius (*Carolus Stuardus*) to be static; Euripides and Lohenstein, however, full of life and passion, make their tragedies dynamic. It is also the great merit of the latter two dramatists to have created and analyzed gigantic women: the plottings of Medea, the cruelty of Electra, the psychologically convincing change in Hecuba from a loving mother into a revenging fury, the whole gamut of passions in Lohenstein's Cleopatra, Sophonisbe, Roxellane, Poppöa. With a clever sense of extremely dramatic stage-effects, they arouse the Aristotelian pity and fear in us. Their heroes, overcome by grief and passion alike, are sometimes on the very brink of degenerating into bloodthirsty criminals. Seneca later was to go to extremes in that development from a strong Ethos to a stark Pathos —and his tragedies (like Lohenstein's *Epicharis*), despite, or because of, their emphasis on stoic teachings, end in slaughter and gore.

Of their Greek contemporaries, probably nobody expressed the difference between Aeschylus and Euripides more clearly than Aristophanes, and he poured scorn on the latter in his *Frogs*. In that play he analyzed the qualities of the two playwrights, pointedly condemned the unfortunate influence of Euripides, and suggested that Aeschylus should arise from Hades to save Athens from internal and external dissolution. In the ensuing dispute of the two tragedians, Euripides began by criticizing the clumsiness of his rival; he boasted, as Lohenstein might have, of having made his style more elegant and fluid, his action more direct, his thoughts more interesting and clear. Aeschylus, however, who exalted Orpheus, Homer and Hesiod, upheld the high moral aims of literature and accused his successor of having failed miserably in training men to be better citizens and worthier human beings. He praised the good old times of faith and discipline; Euripides, he claimed, by glorifying incestuous love and bawds (*Phaedra*), had besmirched the good name of poets who should hide vice from view, and was therefore partly responsible for the demoralization and the godlessness of contemporary youth.

In his *Poetics* Aristotle, too, some sixty years later, found much fault with Euripides, though more on technical than on moral grounds. After calling him "certainly the most tragic of the poets" on account of his pathetic and dynamic conception of the drama, Aristotle, in his *Poetics*, also proceeded to point out Euripides' faults. He blames him for the irrelevancy of his chorus (certainly an outstanding trait also in Lohenstein; e.g. *Ibrahim Bassa*). The chorus is an actor, and should take part in the drama as it did in Sophocles. It should not be detached, and sing interludes that have nothing whatever to do with the plot. The second reproach is directed at the goriness in *Medea*. Pity and fear should be aroused in us by the word only; to show physical monstrosities is inartistic and adds nothing to the catharsis. A third reproach stresses that the characters in Euripides are often needlessly depraved: the heroine in *Electra*, already satirized as a low-peasant woman instead of a princess, becomes a diabolical fury; in *Orestes*, Menelaus is represented as the prototype of the contemptible cowardly tyrant, Helen as a cheap paramour, Orestes as a rowdy and a thief.

It is evident that such parallelisms between Greece and Germany, between Aeschylus-Euripides and Gryphius-Lohenstein, can be accepted only with caution. For, despite the striking similarities in the two struggles between orthodoxy and rationalism and in the evolution of the dramas, there are also vast differences which must not be overlooked. The political unity of the Holy Roman Empire decayed in a slow process which lasted more than five and a half centuries; in Greece, the same disruption took place in fifty years—another example of how rapidly Greek culture grew, flourished and declined. One might also object to the idea of comparing the giants of Greece with Gryphius and Lohenstein, and indeed great honor is done to the two Silesians, although, when an unmistakable general parallel in the development exists, it should not matter much whether we contrast poets of greater or lesser achievements. There is, of course, also the fundamental difference between Aeschylus' dramatic conception of fate and Gryphius' Christian stoicism. Euripides and Lohenstein furthermore both prided themselves on being more fluent in style and action than their predecessors—but here again, Aeschylus' archaic and powerful mode of expression is quite different from Gryphius' heavy, typically baroque style.

It has become customary, since Brunetière's *L'évolution des genres*, to compare cultures or literatures to human beings or seasons, to trees or plants which grow, bloom and decay. The first stage of a culture is a dark mythological beginning; then comes the peak, the golden age of a culture; next, mere civilization; lastly, death. And so Aeschylus, Sophocles and Euripides have been likened to spring, summer and autumn in the history of the Greek tragedy. They show the change from Ethos to Beauty to Pathos; from Aeschylus' heroic style to Sophocles' true classicism, and then to Euripides' naturalism. If we were to accept this interpretation and the corresponding parallel in Germany, then we would have to admit that German literature of the seventeenth century—so characteristically for the Baroque—has only the two extreme forms and that the classicism of Sophocles is missing.

Euripides and Lohenstein used practically the same topics or types of plots as their predecessors—yet a comparison of Sophocles' *Electra* with that of Euripides makes clear the abrupt shift in mentality. The same difference in ethical values may be seen between *e.g.* Gryphius' *Leo Armenius* and Lohenstein's *Ibrahim Sultan*, in the representation of the murdered rulers and those who conspired against them or, in *Katharina von Georgien* and the same play of Lohenstein, in the characterization of the sexually endangered women. All these portrayals are altogether different; in similar circumstances the main characters do not speak the same language at all. Aeschylus and Gryphius, to admonish their fellow-citizens more impressively, chose even contemporary topics to preach against the hybris of Xerxes (*The Persians*) or to condemn the regicide in England (*Carolus Stuardus*). To the original Greek form of the drama, the Christian added one other form which had not existed in Aristotle's times: the martyr-tragedy—unless we think of *Antigone* (as translated by Opitz) as the nearest ancient approach to it. Sophocles' *Antigone* and Gryphius' *Papinianus* both emphasize that god-willed human integrity is more important than any tyrant's laws. The ideal form of the State, according to the poets of the older generation, is an aristocracy or a monarchy abiding by religion and tradition. Aeschylus' *Prometheus* and especially the comedies of Aristophanes fight against the dangers of superficial enlightenment, for the people, only theoretically emancipated, are apt to become an easy prey of demagogues. Gryphius voices exactly the same feelings: his *Stuardus* is a strong protest against revolutions, and Cromwell is as nefarious as Cleon in *The Knights*. In the English event he sides distinctly with the secular ruler against a religious usurper, just as in Leo Armenius his sympathies are with the Byzantinian emperor and not with a presumptuous general. Euripides and Lohenstein, on the other hand, do not believe in monarchs by divine right: Menelaus and Ibrahim Sultan are both criminals and deserve nothing better than death.

The immense difference—not necessarily between Germany and France, but between the mentality and style of Baroque and Classicism—we can also see when we turn to a comparison of the two Silesian playwrights with Corneille and Racine. Whatever cultural ideas Germany (or, for that matter, England) appropriated from seventeenth-century France especially in literature, came into a very different cultural milieu and were distorted accordingly. The pseudo-classical rules regarding style, meter and dramatic technicalities could be imitated outwardly, it is true; but the essential poise, delicacy and psychological depth of courtly French literature were beyond the capabilities of all other European writers of that century. If French authors imitated Spanish or Italian models, these imitations, in the hands of Corneille or of Molière, became new masterpieces; if the Germans (or Sir John Denham or Shadwell) imitated the French, their works became mere parodies. Germany in the post-war period after 1648 lacked all the things that made for great literature: she had no theatres, no critics, no actors, no public of any consequence. French literary art could build upon what Ronsard, Garnier and Malherbe had achieved, and could discipline itself by the dignified rules of the newly founded *Académie Française*. But Germany had no such traditions, no such cultural centers as Paris or Versailles. Thus an examination of the ethical and aesthetic standards of the French and the German drama shows more clearly than anything else the cultural abyss that separated the two nations around 1660. Such a comparison will demonstrate how far literary excellence depends upon suitable environmental conditions, and how many and what manner of social factors—present in classical France, absent in baroque Germany—have to contribute to its quality. Given a certain plot, the German and the French dramatists approached it from different angles, with different methods, with different purposes in view; they emphasized, deleted, changed and intensified incidents in accordance with their respective ethical and aesthetic principles.

We can be brief about Gryphius' martyr-tragedies and their gloomy end in the utter defeat of the cause of God *e.g.* in *Katharina*. The two martyr-tragedies by Corneille, *Polyeucte* and *Théodore* end in a much more hopeful tone, for the Frenchman's Catholic doctrine of divine grace works miracles among former pagans who have observed the sufferings and the steadfastness of Polyeucte and Néarque, and the concluding lines indicate that quite a few among these heathens will become Christian. Not so the Protestant Gryphius: his piling up of horrors and tortures may end in the ultimate insanity of the villainous ruler of Persia, Chach Abas, but it is not weakened through miraculous last-minute conversions (except, possibly, in *Felicitas*, a Jesuit drama which Gryphius translated from the French Father Causinus). With regard only to the treatment of love and sex was Gryphius more discreet than Corneille, for in his *Vorrede* to *Leo Armenius* he reproached the author of *Polyeucte* for having mixed love and religion in that play. Later, Corneille went even further and spoke of the sexual assault on Théodore, a *faux pas* in increasingly classical France for which his contemporaries made him pay dearly, even though he had treated this particular passage with great delicacy. In comparing the two authors we can also say that in his tragedies Gryphius ardently remained loyal to martyr-plays for the rest of his life, while Corneille soon forsook this genre for other themes. The religious fervor of the *renaissance catholique*, so strong under

Louis XIII, was waning rapidly, and the Paris of Louis XIV was much more interested in portrayals of intrigue and passion. Although, in the 1650's, Corneille kept up his religious interests to the point, for instance, of translating Thomas à Kempis' *Imitatio Christi*, he did not revert to religious themes in his later tragedies, even though a play like *Attila* would have given him an excellent opportunity—for its plot, so similar to Gryphius' *Katharina*, shows the cruel necessity for a Christian princess to marry a pagan, barbarian conqueror. Still, the mere existence of *Polyeucte* and *Théodore* gives us enough reason to compare Corneille with Gryphius and to assert that both men, who lived during the time of the Thirty Years' War and of the Fronde, were of a similarly hard and heroic mentality and that, in contrast to the later Racine and Lohenstein, they showed us, in a grandiose and cumbersome fashion, men not as they ordinarily are, weak and unprincipled, but as they ought to be in moments of great exaltation: strong, sublime, impervious to all sufferings and compromises.

To turn now to Lohenstein, who presented crimes and butcheries for their own sake, caring naught about religion or integrity and dwelling merely on human passions at their worst: nobody would really dare to compare him with that other great painter of passions, Racine, because the German was totally unable to show the subtle workings of a human soul. Indeed, he shows only volcanic eruptions, fortissimo-episodes, leaping from peak to peak in his plots, without having Racine's fine gift of tracing his heroes' motives and character changes. The restrained classicist would employ a probing monologue to reveal some frightful crisis or to lead to a grand climax, whereas the still baroque Lohenstein uses physical tortures, rapes and other horrors for such a situation. This tendency to show everything from the worst possible angle shows itself already in his first tragedy, *Ibrahim Bassa*, in which, —in contrast to his models, Mlle de Scudéry's novel and Zesen's German translation of it —the hero indeed became the victim of the treacherous casuistry of the Sultan Soliman who was lusting after Ibrahim's wife Isabella.

Lohenstein's second Turkish tragedy, *Ibrahim Sultan*, may well be cited as a contrast to Racine's *Bajazet*, in order to underscore the abyss even more. Both rulers were the surviving brothers of Amurat IV who had exterminated most of his family and was soon to die in 1640. Psychology or would-be psychology, intrigues, passions and harem-murders play a great role in both works. Yet here again we see the great difference between the Frenchman and the German: where Racine shows real psychological dilemmas that express themselves in thoughts rather than in actions, in restrained words rather than in bombast, Lohenstein is capable of showing only despicable deeds of violence. Bajazet, sentenced to death by the sultan, his brother, and yet conspiring against him, is loved by two women, one of whom will betray him and his conspiracy to Amurat and cause his execution if he does not reciprocate her passion. For Racine, this constant dilemma, these effects and counter-effects of Bajazet's affections, are the whole *raison d'être* of this psychologically penetrating tragedy about a man who has to choose between life and love; and the author is not greatly interested in the fact that in the end three of the four main characters are killed. Racine referred only disdainfully to the youngest brother, calling him "l'imbécile Ibrahim" — but this psychopath now, of course, became the main hero and monster for a man like Lohenstein, who showed him in the very first scene in an attempted rape of the widow of his dead brother Amurat. We need not say more about Lohenstein's portrayal of the "unspeakable Turk" to stress its basic difference from the fine emotional chess-game played in Racine's *Bajazet*.

If we now turn to Lohenstein's two African tragedies, *Sophonisbe* and *Cleopatra*, we perceive again that the former differs greatly from the outstanding French version of the seventeenth century, Mairet's tragedy of 1634. The story, found in the thirtieth book of Livy and again in the fifth canto of Petrarch's epic *Africa*, was crude and immoral, yet bluntly accurate, in Trissino's famous first Italian neo-classical tragedy of 1515. Mairet now tried to improve on this by eliminating the two most offensive details, bigamy and sycophancy: first, Syphax, Sophonisbe's first husband, dies in battle and the queen does not marry Massinisse until some time afterwards and thus does not become guilty of bigamy; and second, Massinisse kills himself after Sophonisbe's suicide, and thus appears as a tender and faithful lover rather than as an obedient ally and vassal of victorious Rome. Not so Lohenstein: his Massinissa, a contemptible opportunist who had willingly extradited his mistress to the Romans, is richly rewarded by Scipio—and as to Sophonisbe's calculating ensnaring of him, as long as there was a chance that he might save her against Rome, there could be no doubt about her intentions, even though her husband Syphax was still alive and in captivity.

Naturally enough, the German, with his interest in gigantic, passionate characters, was attracted also by that other *femme fatale*, Cleopatra. In increasingly restrained France, it must be said, the interest had begun to turn away from her purely sexual misdeeds. Mairet, in his *Marc Antoine*, dwelled rather on Marc Antony, his career, his character, and his political problems, while Corneille in *La mort de Pompée* showed, not the passionate love-affairs of Cleopatra, but the great historical background of Roman-Egyptian relations and described the momentous turning-point in Roman history when Pompey, after the defeat at Pharsalia, was murdered in Egypt at Caesar's behest and when Cleopatra, the favorite of Caesar, became queen of Egypt. Both Frenchmen thus approached an old, worn topic from a new angle: Corneille made it a grand historical spectacle, and Mairet an analysis of a statesman torn between conjugal love for Octavia and fatal infatuation for Cleopatra. For Lohenstein, however, the over-emphasis on eroticism was still good enough. He did not introduce pompous historical displays, but dwelled exclusively on the scheming, fighting and intriguing of his lascivious heroine who was willing, as Sophonisbe had been, to accept any lover able to help her against annexation by Rome and who, even at the sight of the corpse of Mark Antony, could not refrain from making revoltingly sensual remarks about past amorous delights enjoyed with the dead man.

But is is in Lohenstein's two Roman tragedies, *Agrippina* and *Epicharis*, that the awesome difference between baroque and classical treatments of historical topics is most evident. Any reader will be aware of the wonderful discretion in Racine's *Britannicus*, a tragedy which shows Nero standing at the crossroads of good and evil, deliberating whether or not he should commit his first murder, that of Britannicus, and thus turn from the innocence of his youth to the viciousness of his manhood. That moment of pondering hesitation is all that matters to Racine; not the later crimes of this man. After Britannicus' death, Agrippina merely alludes to what may come later:

> "Mais j'espère qu'enfin le ciel, las de tes crimes
> Ajoutera ta perte à tant d'autres victimes...
> Et ton nom paraîtra, dans la race future
> Aux plus cruels tyrans une cruelle injure."

More Racine is not prepared to say. But that is, of course, the starting-point of the still baroque and blunt Lohenstein who reaches a new nadir in the third act of *Agrippina*, when the old woman, in order to regain some power over her son, with rationalistic sophistry tries to persuade Nero to become her lover.

Epicharis, the story of a conspiracy against Nero, has a telling counterpart in Corneille's *Cinna*. In each play a woman, Epicharis in the former, Emilie in the latter, is the leader of the conspiracy. Both of them plot against a much-hated Roman emperor, and both, by promises of love or by sheer oratory, inveigle various men into helping to execute their plans. In both tragedies the conspiracy is betrayed by disappointed suitors, and the guilty ones are caught. At this point we see again the immense difference, not so much between German and French, as between baroque and classical endings for such a situation. Corneille's aim is to study and portray superhuman and noble characters; in a magnificent fifth act he shows us how Augustus can finally conquer his natural desire for revenge and how, after a heroic ethical effort, he can forgive Emilie and her lover Cinna:

> "Je suis maître de moi, comme de l'univers;
> Je le suis, je veux l'être....
> Soyons amis, Cinna."

It would have been not only beyond the intention, but also beyond the ability, of Lohenstein to devise such an ending. What he presents is hatred, bestiality, mass executions and tortures of the worst kind – butcheries in the case of *Epicharis* just as revolting as Nero's sexual perversity in *Agrippina*.

Racine, in his second preface to *Britannicus*, was loath to say too much;

after referring briefly to Agrippina's ferociousness, he merely remarks significantly: "Je ne dis que ce mot d'Agrippine, car il y aurait trop de choses à en dire." Here is classical discretion at its finest—a trait which was simply beyond the comprehension of a man like Lohenstein. Germany had to wait another hundred years before that message from France, as well as the Greek gospel of "noble simplicity and quiet grandeur," began to take roots in her literature.

X. SOME GERMAN CONTRIBUTIONS TO
EUROPEAN LITERATURE[1]

In spite of the dangers inherent in making broad generalizations about national traits and national literatures—because most thoughtful listeners can easily think of many minor exceptions which seem to contradict such generalizations—it is, at times, quite fascinating and thought-provoking to stress certain national literary trends, because they help to clarify the broad over-all picture of European literature. I beg you, therefore, to accept some of my contentions with a grain of salt and I only hope that you will agree with me that the canvas painted with a few bold strokes (though it may disregard certain finer shadings) nevertheless conjures up a picture of German traits and contributions which is essentially accurate. In trying to evaluate some of these contributions, I shall very often have occasion to compare German literature with French literature, for these two nations to me represent the two most important antitheses in Western European letters. Neither England nor Spain, nor even Italy, can as clearly and unequivocally serve as leaders of the Germania and Romania (to use one of Fritz Strich's favorite antitheses) as can Germany and France. To study the characteristics and the differences of these two countries means, in a way, to study the quintessence of Western civilization. Happily enough, the French and German minds do not only vie with each other, and compete with each other, as it were, for the first place in European letters; they also complement each other, each one having some of the very traits and values which the other lacks—and in their better moments there takes place between the two nations a most fruitful exchange of ideas and ideals

---

[1]Address delivered as one of three "Lectures in the Humanities" in Chapel Hill, November 1949 and reprinted from the 6th Series of the *UNC Extension Bulletin*, XXX, 1950, 6-20.

which is all the more important because the fate of the political as well as of the cultural relations between France and Germany very often contributes to the determination of the destiny of Western Europe as a whole. The pendulum of Europe's intellectual leadership swings constantly between Romania and Germania, between France and Germany; and thus the life of European literature may indeed be compared to a living organism, to a great lung, which is now inhaling and now exhaling, now accepting the standards of France and now again accepting the values of Germany.

And what are these different traits between which Europe is constantly oscillating? I suppose one of the easiest ways to define the two is to say that France is the home of Classicism and Germany the home of Romanticism. It is not the time or the place to elaborate here in detail on the essence of these two -isms; may it suffice to state that Classicism, in spite of its Italian origins, found the most perfect expression in the France of 1660, because its ideals of reason, restraint, dignity, rules and decorum were thoroughly germane to the flower of French society. Not so the essentially irrational and romantic mentality of the Germans, who want originality instead of imitation, spectacularness instead of restraint, faith and ardor instead of scepticism, fantasy instead of verisimilitude, nature instead of civilization, individualism instead of etiquette, the heart instead of the brain. The result is well known: the masters of French Classicism found only a weak and miserable echo in Germany around 1740 because the Germans resented French Neo-Classicism as something thoroughly alien to their mind, and the leaders of German Romanticism found a belated and short-lived echo in France between 1827 and 1843 because the classical French instinctively felt that Romanticism was alien to them, too. Foreign values may for a while be superimposed upon a nation, yet sooner or later every nation will revert to its own inherent characteristics.

Classical Romania and romantic Germania — that means, if we carry the above characterizations a little farther, that France is static and Germany dynamic, that the one builds the form, the law, the society, the state, and that the other breaks it. To the Germans, the status quo means retrogression, perhaps even death; forever they grope blindly forward, towards – who knows? – a better future, smashing the semi-permanent fixtures the French put in their way, like the Phoenix forever feeling the restless urge to die and to arise again from its ashes. Mankind must necessarily consist of these two parts: of the one element that strikes out in ever-new directions, never satisfied with that which is, but always anxious to grope for that which will be – and of the other element which is calmer, maturer perhaps, and which consolidates what has been achieved and is reluctant to embark upon tempestuous new adventures.

We can watch this fascinating rhythm between dynamic Germania and restraining Romania in the history of the past 1500 years, from the moment when the Romania built the Roman state, Roman law and Roman society and when invading Germanic tribes, in the fifth century, smashed all this and replaced the unity of the civilized world by a chaotic medley of small Germanic kingdoms. Then, from 800 till 1250, the pendulum swung back to law and order again: Charlemagne established the Holy Roman Empire and created new unity; the growing age of French chivalry propagated certain ideals of etiquette and restraint; literature gropingly found its way back to fluency, delicacy, style; and scholasticism held in its firm embrace both the religion and the philosophy of that age. By 1250, however, there followed the new disintegration: the slow decay of the Empire, the Peasant Rebellions in England and Germany, the rise of the bourgeoisie, the disappearance of chivalrous norms, the defeat of scholasticism at the hands of the German mystics, the decline of the Papacy, and – the crowning event in this slow progress of emancipation and disintegration – the Lutheran schism in 1517. Yet in that very same period the pendulum began to swing back to the Romania, to order, discipline, dignity and formalism: the beauties of the Italian Renaissance, the revival of Antiquity through the humanists, the trend towards political absolutism in France, Spain, England, the splendor of courtly society, the golden age of French Classicism. And by 1750, of course, there began again the Germanic counterthrust, English Pre-Romanticism, the German Storm and Stress, the political, literary and emotional emancipation of the Romantic Age. To this very day we witness the same rhythm between ebb and flood, between reason and impulse, between consolidating France and dynamic Germany—an inhaling and an exhaling comparable indeed to the workings of a lung, one as fully needed as the other.

Classical Romania and romantic Germania: that opens up vistas into many other literary differences, too. It means, for instance, that the French are essentially strong in intellectual and analytical literature, in works composed rationally, painstakingly, almost scientifically, in their stylistic perfection, whereas the Germans distinguish themselves by individualistic, lyrical, emotional outpourings. French Classicism excels in the tragedy (that most mathematical of all genres), the social comedy of manners, the satire, the philosophical essay or novel, the epigram and in any other type of literature that permits a careful analysis of men, manners and times. This atmosphere of objective picturization was further enhanced by the typically classical system of rules, concerning unities, meter, catharsis and decorum that pervaded the age of Louis XIV and of Voltaire. Not so the Germans: for them romantic stammerings, lyrical outbursts, individual confessions and fragmentary shreds of stanzas, chapters and scenes seem far more important than calmly detached analyses of society. France is pre-eminently social-minded, as evidenced, above all, by the Revolution of 1789 which, because of the very character and the political maturity of the French people, had to be the great contribution of France to the history of European thought. Not so the German poet, who cares little about the structure of the state and his own place in society and who does not, by the very nature of his mystical calling, care for social satires, witty epigrams, dainty madrigals and courtly celebrations. German literature at its best is personal, lyrical, irrational; and it is certainly no mere coincidence that this typically German trait shows itself not only in the great number of its lyrical poets but also in the outstanding quality of its musical composers. In music and in lyrical poetry, Germany conquered for herself a field which Europe had hardly ever touched upon—for, though the France of the seventeenth and eighteenth centuries had her Lully, her La Fontaine and her Chénier, she had nothing that could compare with the lyrics of Klopstock, Bürger, Goethe, Novalis, Eichendorff or Heine, nor with the music of Beethoven and Brahms or the songs of Schubert and Schumann.

German literature is so essentially personal that even German novels manage to attain a lyrical ring. Usually a novel is broad and objective, more often than not (as, for instance, in Balzac and Zola, or in the Spanish picaresque tale) giving us a tableau of the social conditions of an entire nation or of individual strata within human society. Not so the average German novel with its constant emphasis on individual problems: it dwells on the soul of one human being alone, delineates its development in all its minute aspects, and includes a picture of human society at large only insofar as that is necessary to the description of the problems and the potentialities of the one chosen hero or heroine. Hence the growth and popularity of that eminently German type of novel, the "Bildungsroman" or apprenticeship novel, which depicts the growth of the soul of a human being and its quest for a valid philosophy of life, from the innocence of youth to the wisdom of old age. Wolfram von Eschenbach's *Parzival* was the first great medieval respresentative of this kind of novel showing Parzival's quest of the Holy Grail, his persevering, stumbling and succeeding, in spite of the follies, disappointments and failures of his youth. With Grimmelshausen's *Simplizissimus*, the outstanding German novel of the seventeenth century, the scene of the apprenticeship of the human being was shifted from the romantic chivalry of the Arthurian Age to the realism, the obscenity and the depravity of the Thirty Years' War — yet here, too, Simplizissimus, the hero, after a life of sin and crime, ultimately found the path to God and to inner peace. With Wieland's *Agathon*, one of the finest German novels of the eighteenth century, the goal of the apprenticeship shifted from divine to human happiness, for Agathon, after many errors, was finally to find peace in a gently epicurean philosophy of life, and in the love of an ideal woman. Goethe's *Wilhelm Meister*, commonly hailed as the greatest of all German apprenticeship novels, showed that independent individualism, hitherto so dear to German poets and thinkers, could not survive in the nineteenth century of social strife and civic responsibility, for Wilhelm, after a rather aimless life as *bel-esprit* and wayfaring actor, ended up as a surgeon, an ideal profession, not only because it combines perfectly the skills of the brain with the dexterity of the hand, but also because it gave Wilhelm a chance to live and work for the benefit of the greatest possible number of fellow-beings.

The German apprenticeship novels of the nineteenth and twentieth centuries, from Novalis, Tieck and Mörike on, are too numerous to be mentioned here. Instead, I should like to point to a sub-species of this type of individual soul-searching which is particularly popular with the German authors of our war-stricken twentieth century: the theme of "Wandlung," of a sudden inner regeneration, of a spiritual rebirth of the hero. Russians like Tolstoy may originally have been responsible for this theme which showed how the hero, under the tremendous impact of some great event, suddenly revaluated all concepts and strove for a complete reorientation of his life and an ennobling of his ideals; but the very idea appealed so much to the individualism and mysticism-loving Germans that "Wandlung," or regeneration, helped not only to enrich the vast field of apprenticeship novels (*e.g.* Jakob Wassermann's *Christian Wahnschaffe*, known in English under the title of *The World's Illusion*), but it was taken over also into the field of the expressionistic drama (*e.g.* with Ernst Toller) and of lyrical poetry (*e.g.* with Rainer Maria Rilke and Franz Werfel).

Another most characteristic trait of the Germans we must mention here is the religious turn their individualistic speculations customarily take. Religion is so deeply embedded in the German frame of thinking that already Mme de Staël exclaimed that German northern Protestantism was really much more earnestly and genuinely religious than the glittering formalism of Southern European Catholicism. This steadfast religious preoccupation can best be seen in the German history of the sixteenth and seventeenth centuries, for, whereas the word Renaissance for Italy, France and even England meant an aesthetic, a literary, a philosophical rebirth, it could mean nothing but a religious rebirth, a spiritual regeneration, for the Germans. Let the Italians bother about such vain things as the smoothness of Petrarch's sonnets, the accomplishments of Castiglione's *Courtier*, or the perfection of Leonardo da Vinci's art; let Francis I transform Fontainebleau into a glittering center of French Renaissance culture; or let Elizabethans like Raleigh and Drake give vent to their proud Renaissance vigorousness by becoming buccaneering empire-builders in lands across the seas. For the Germans there was no problem more important than the road back to God, the re-establishment of the ideals of the Church Fathers, the *reformatio* and *regeneratio* of institution and individual alike, even though it means schism, religious wars, death and ultimately also the destruction of the German Empire. Of the three leading events in the history of modern European thought, Italy had her aesthetic Renaissance, France three centuries later had her political Revolution, and Germany, not really concerned with either of these two aspects of life, had her religious Reformation. It could not be otherwise.

Nor were these constant religious ponderings restricted to the teachings of Luther, the mysticism of Böhme, the martyr-tragedies of Gryphius, the *Theodicy* of Leibniz, the theological deliberations of Schleiermacher, or the doubts of Strauss and Feuerbach. Modern authors also, apprentices all in man's heartbreaking struggle for a really valid philosophy of life, are, in the last analysis, God-seekers – not only Rilke, Werfel and Wassermann, whom I would count among the finest authors of our time, but also Hermann Stehr in his *Heiligenhof Farm*, Gustav Frenssen in *Jörn Uhl*, Max Brod in *Tycho Brahe's Road to God*, or Erwin Guido Kolbenheyer in his *Paracelsus* and in *Master Joachim Pausewang*. The hero of such an inner regeneration, like Christian Wahnschaffe in Wassermann's novel by the same title, will be apt to give up his father's wealth and luxury, descend into the slums and become the friend and the helper of the weak and the oppressed, yes indeed of harlots, criminals and other outcasts – a new Buddha, a new Christ, to go out among the lepers. No wonder that, in the face of all this, urbane Frenchmen like Henri Massis, in his challenging book *La Défense de l'Occident*, claimed that level-headed France alone was the guardian of Western civilization, because Asia with its oriental mysticism and its muddle-headed communism extended to the very borders of the Rhine! And, as if replying to such taunts by Western materialists, Gerhart Hauptmann in his fascinating novel *The Fool in Christ, Emmanuel Quint*, asks just what would befall Christ if He were born again into this modern, cynical Western world of ours. Would not He too be scorned, rejected, vilified, locked up in an insane asylum as Emmanuel Quint was? An endless preoccupation with religion, an indefatigable quest of God, we find even where God seems to be enigmatic, cruel and elusive rather than kindly, helpful and forgiving, as, for instance, in Franz Kafka's *The Trial*.

And the road to God, to his own personal concept of God, every German must find alone, for nobody can help him in this hardest of all human tasks. That had been the greatest deed of Luther, that he tore every individual out of the protective hierarchy of the Catholic Church and made him face his Creator, the problem of his salvation, alone. How much better off was Dante, that most typical of all Catholic God-seekers, who, on his eventful trip through the three realms of the beyond, had Virgil and Cato and then Beatrice to help him, to explain, assist and warn him, to prevent him from falling by the wayside, and to urge him on until at long last he reached the sight of God! Not so Parzival (originally a foreign tale to which the Germans have given an unusually deep religious meaning) who, a Protestant long before Luther, had to stumble and struggle on alone in his quest of the Holy Grail, like his English fellow-Protestant, Christian, in Bunyan's *Pilgrim's Progress*, without a guide to direct and comfort him. And even much worse off than he was that greatest of all German seekers of truth, Faust, who not only had no guide, no Virgil, to lead him, but who had at all times at his side a Mephistopheles purposely to mislead him. Yet in spite of this deadly handicap, even Faust ended up by finding his God, his philosophy of life, for, in the words of Goethe, he who aspires unweariedly is not beyond redeeming, and a human soul, through obscurest aspirations, is always aware of the one right path and, after many pitfalls and temptations, will surely revert to it.

As we look at this nation of restless seekers, we suddenly become aware of the fact that for most of them the searching, the progressing, the expanding are far more important than the finding and possessing. Faust, dissatisfied, dynamic, onward-rushing all his life, realized this fact very well when he stated in a significant line that possession makes lazy — and contented, static, indolent and smug he vows he will never be. For Lessing, too, the searching and stumbling were far more important than the finding and the self-indulgent enjoying; hence his immortal and beautiful statement to the effect that if God held in his right hand absolute Truth and in his left hand man's everlasting hunger for Truth, though with the stipulation that this hunger should never be satisfied and that man should always err in his search, and if God then said "Choose!," he, Lessing, would humbly fall into God's left arm and say: "Father, give—for absolute Truth is for Thee alone."

This statement incidentally indicates also that Lessing, commonly called the greatest of all German enlighteners, was not really an enlightener in the strict French sense of the word, because for rationalists like Voltaire there were few, if any, dark corners left in this universe that were not capable of being investigated and illuminated by man's keen intellectual analysis—whereas Lessing, a German and hence a mystic after all, was quite willing to admit that the ultimate answers to many questions lie with God and not with man. Let us not forget either that, after the heyday of French sensualism and materialism around 1750, it was a German philosopher, Immanuel Kant, who sternly proclaimed the existence of metaphysical concepts which, to be sure, may transcend human experience, rationalism and provability, but are none the less real, valid and eternal. Just as we previously emphasized that, because of the lyrical and emotional qualities of German literature, it was not a coincidence that German music also reached such world-famed heights, so now we can emphasize, too, that this searching, speculative, metaphysical trait of the German character was likewise naturally conducive to placing the Germans—Kant, Hegel, Schelling and others—among the foremost philosophers of modern Europe.

Other qualities of German literature can be deduced from the broad traits outlined above. Being an individualist, given to dreams, visions, hopes and passions of his own, the German poet will not usually be a sociable person or a courtier. Other poets and literatures may be deeply rooted in the life of a brilliant court: Castiglione at Urbino, Ariosto at Ferrara, the Elizabethans in London, Calderón in Madrid, the great French classicists in the Paris and Versailles of Louis XIV. Not so the Germans, who prefer isolation, who want to go their own ways, who feel clumsy and constrained when forced into a social pattern. Classical France, the product of a brilliant society, and believing in rules, dignity and decorum, had found it relatively easy in the days of Richelieu to establish the *Académie française*, which became the supreme lawgiver and umpire in all matters pertaining to literature. Such coordination would have been unthinkable in the very loose republic of German letters in which each poet wished to follow his own ideals — and when, almost 300 years after Richelieu, there was finally established in Germany a feeble imitation of the French Academy, it distinguished itself, in the days of the Weimar Republic, mainly by the fact that most of the leading German authors refused to belong to it; and in the days of the Third Reich it displayed a more or less complete sterility. German literature has never flourished in a socially or politically compact state; it blossomed forth in the eighteenth century, when the Empire consisted of an exasperating medley of 300 individual Lilliputian states, one smaller, quainter and more picturesque than the other; it reached its unsurpassed Golden Age during the twenty-five years from the French Revolution to Waterloo, when the political unity of Germany had completely ceased to exist and the whole country lay prostrate under the heel of Napoleon; and its abundant regional literature in Mecklenburg, Schleswig-Holstein, Westphalia, Swabia and Silesia in the later nineteenth century could thrive only because even then Berlin was only the political, and not the cultural, capital of the Reich.

Of course, there was the one great exception, the exception to prove the rule, as it were: Goethe — the poet who did become a courtier, a political and a social figure and who, as Prime Minister, ruled for several years over the little duchy of Saxony-Weimar. Yet in his *Torquato Tasso*, perhaps the most autobiographical of his many autobiographical works, he everlastingly told of the tragedy, the incompatibility, the impossibility of being a poet and a courtier at the same time. For Goethe at the court of Weimar and for Tasso at the court of Ferrara, to be a gifted and sensitive genius among the smooth conventions, the intrigues and the materialistic opportunism of courtiers, was too much to be borne. No wonder that in the case of Tasso the impossible situation ended in utter tragedy; he was hurt, offended, stifled in his divine inspiration and finally driven to insanity. Goethe's own strong character was able to avoid a similar catastrophe, but for his German fellow-poets the message of this tragedy was none the less clear: do not ever become a courtier;

117

instead, remain loyal to your great calling, even though the cost of greatness may be isolation and loneliness.

And, speaking of Goethe, let us add that he and Schiller were the two great exceptions in a second regard also, for he and Schiller alone, in the midst of an essentially romantic Germany, all of a sudden became classicists — Greek rather than French classicists, though — and began to proclaim the validity of those very same classical concepts which the German romanticists thought they had killed off long ago. Yet it has frequently been pointed out — and correctly, I think — that Goethe's greatest fame rests upon those of his works which are either completely romantic (the lyricism of his Storm and Stress poems, the emotionalism of his *Werther*) or which hide a classical message in a thoroughly romantic form (*Faust, Wilhelm Meister, The Elective Affinities*). If Goethe in his maturity became far more classical than this fellow-Germans wanted him to be, it was simply because he in his wisdom clearly recognized the great dangers of too much romanticism, emotionalism, mysticism and Germanism, and hence in *Wilhelm Meister* he preached that an apprenticeship novel should actually culminate in a sound education and should not lose itself merely in a wild romantic butterfly-chasing and in visionary hallucinations. In *Faust*, he postulated that civic responsibility, in the last analysis, was far more important than unbridled individualism; in *The Elective Affinities* he spoke up against adulterous passions among foot-loose romanticists which undermine the very cornerstone of modern society, just as in other works of this period he warned against the blind, deadly hatred of the masses for Napoleon's France, and, after life's trials and tribulations had weakened the romanticists, against their cowardly surrender of their Lutheran integrity and intellectual freedom to the tenets of the Catholic Church. Our own age has come to realize to what horrible aberrations German Romanticism could lead, when emotionalism became frenzy and mysticism became racism, and Goethe was among the first Germans who tried to apply the brakes when he realized what the resulting excesses of all this might be.

All his words about self-discipline, restraint and reason were, however, of no avail, for around Goethe the romantic poets increasingly developed a typically German and romantic trait: "Weltschmerz." It was a tragedy, not only to be a poet among courtiers, as Goethe's *Tasso* had indicated, but to be a poet among materialistic, indifferent, acquisitive mankind in general. Hence now the great number of misfits in German literature, poets who suffer from world-grief, who, like some of Thomas Mann's favorite characters, do not fit in anywhere, do not belong, feel repelled by the increasing soullessness of an industrialized world. Goethe's own *Werther*, written as early as 1773, became the ancestor of a whole tribe of gifted, sensitive weaklings at home and abroad, whose increasing despair drove them either into insanity (Hölderlin, Lenau), suicide (Kleist), voluntary exile (Heine, Platen), or who otherwise managed to lead a thoroughly miserable and frustrated life (Grillparzer, Mörike), to embrace the comforting message of the Catholic Church (Stolberg, Schlegel, Werner) or to die a premature death (Novalis, Wackenroder). It is not the place here to speak of similar *Weltschmerz*-poets in other lands; suffice it to state that Germany, the homeland of Romanticism, was much more affected by a multitude of such tragic misfits. Werther, Faust, Ahasverus the Wandering Jew —all became symbols of restless and despairing seekers of happiness; even Don Juan was thrown in for good measure in a fascinating tragedy on *Faust and Don Juan* by Christian Grabbe, where the one, the seeker of the spirit, and the other, the seeker of the flesh, are shown together in their heartbreaking journey through life. And again, as so often in the history of German culture, music and philosophy support a basic trend found in German literature—I need refer only to Wagner's *Flying Dutchman*, who, doomed to sail the Seven Seas to all eternity, despaired of ever finding peace; or to the abysmal pessimism in Schopenhauer's philosophy, formulated in 1819, in the midst of this romantic convulsion.

Metaphysical speculations and aimless dreaminess and melancholy and other traits so dear to exaggerated Romanticism showed themselves also in other aspects of German literature. There is, for example, the Blue Flower, the famous symbol of the romantic apprenticeship novel, the goal of the vague and undefinable aspirations of Heinrich von Ofterdingen, the hero of Novalis' novel by the same name, who, unlike

Goethe's Wilhelm Meister, never did finish his apprenticeship and never did find the Blue Flower and whatever it may have stood for. There is also the typical German yearning for death—another result of that romantic twilight-atmosphere of dreams and hallucinations—a trend which is very marked in Novalis' *Hymns to the Night*, and continues to our present age of Rilke and Hesse. Thomas Mann in his *Magic Mountain* has perhaps most convincingly portrayed this strange lure of death among the members of an over-ripe, tired civilization idling away their remaining days in a Swiss sanatorium in the Alps—though it must be admitted, too, that in the last chapters of the novel, the hero, Hans Castorp, has the strength to break away from that seductive mountain of death and to plan to return to an active role in life—only, most likely, to find death a few weeks later, on the battlefields of 1914. And a third symbol attractive to the German romanticists especially during those hazy decades after the destruction of the First Reich by Napoleon in 1806 when the Germans, amidst their dreamy, idealistic speculations so dear to the mind of an observant traveler like Mme de Staël, failed to face the realities and to show the physical strength and determination to establish a new, a Second, Reich: they thought their entire nation resembled Prince Hamlet, an idealist and dreamer too good for the cruel necessities of this world. The fashion of dwelling on the basically Hamlet-like character especially of Central and Southern Germany lent itself to many pleasant speculations and parallelisms until the Prussians took over in 1834, in 1866, and in 1871, and put a rude end to such idle philosophizing.

To continue with other typical traits of German literature: the German poets, in their constant preoccupation with the problems, dreams, ambitions and idiosyncrasies of one great individual, soon came to treat frequently the tragic problem of the hero who had overstepped himself and was not as great or superhuman a figure as he had assumed he was. I am not speaking here of the numberless ill-fated rebels of Storm and Stress literature (Prometheus, Götz von Berlichingen, Faust, Karl Moor), nor of false pretenders of the type of Schiller's Demetrius; instead, I should like to point to heroes or heroines who were born into greatness and leadership, yet, like Goethe's Tasso, were not strong enough to pay the exorbitant price of all greatness, namely loneliness. Take Schiller's *Maid of Orleans*, supposedly a divine figure, strong, superhuman, the God-inspired leader and deliverer of an entire nation who, however, in Schiller's version, at the critical moment discovered that she was a weak mortal after all. She, of all people, fell in love on the battlefield with an English enemy of France and in her own eyes she was therefore now a failure, a leader who had betrayed her divine mission and so deserved to die. The same holds true for Kleist's Penthesilea and for Grillparzer's Sappho, too, both supposedly great and immortal figures — the one the tough queen of the Amazons, the other one of the great, detached and priestlike bards of Greece — yet both at a critical moment really lovesick females, without pride or dignity, who resolve to atone for their weakness and shame by seeking voluntary death. Greatness means loneliness almost beyond endurance: Wagner's Lohengrin also, the keeper of the Holy Grail, had to learn this bitter truth, when, in spite of his God-like mission, he yearned for the companionship of a mortal woman; and Heinrich, the hero in Hauptmann's *Sunken Bell*, experienced the same conflict and tragic end when he realized what the heartbreaking implications of his exclusive devotion to art would be.

The position of womanhood in modern Germany may leave much to be desired — but there is no doubt, astonishing though it may sound, that in German literature woman holds a place of respect and importance second to none in modern civilization. Already Tacitus in his *Germania* had marveled at the high esteem of women among the old Germanic tribes, and it cannot be emphasized sufficiently that the two great national epics of the German Middle Ages were devoted to two great women alone: Kriemhilde and Gudrun. Other heroic sagas of Europe — *Roland, Beowulf, the Cid, Alexander* — deal essentially with man's world, with bloody wars and daring adventures. Not so the *Nibelungen Song* which, in spite of all slaughters and blood-curdling cruelties, is again, in so typical a German fashion, the story of just one great individual, this time a woman, Kriemhilde. External events, intrigues, treachery and massacres (we feel as we read and reread this epic) are not the main thing for our unknown author; what he wants to show above all, lovingly and in detail, is the soul of this important woman. He explains, in delicate stages, just how and why she changed from a tender, innocent maiden into a loving bride of Siegfried, a mature woman, a loyal wife, and how and why, after her husband's foul assassination, she was gradually transformed from a mourning widow into a frenzied, revengeful fury who, in her sadistic rage, caused the deaths of tens of thousands of her fellow-Burgundians in order to avenge the death of her man. And just as in the *Nibelungen* a woman's supreme loyalty to her mate had shown itself in frightful hatred and wholesale killings, so in the second German national epic, *Gudrun*, a woman's loyalty showed itself in supreme faith, patience and endurance. Gudrun is incomparably more modern than the semi-barbarian Kriemhilde; even though she was kidnapped by a rejected suitor and for thirteen long years was kept in miserable captivity and humiliation a in storm-swept castle on the North Sea, Gudrun reacted passively rather than actively, preserving her womanly attributes of faith, hope, gentleness and chastity until at last she was found and delivered by the man she loved. Of the author's genuine respect and admiration for the valor and the loyalty of these two great women there can be no doubt.

Centuries later, at the peak of German Idealism, with Wieland, Schiller, and especially Goethe, woman was to occupy an even more exalted place in German literature. Goethe's *Iphigenia* is surely unsurpassed in this respect, for it portrays a thoroughly christianized heroine who through the nobility, the piety and the purity of her character alone saved herself, her frenzied brother Orestes and her curse-ridden family from doom and damnation. It is Goethe's immortal monument of gratitude for the ennobling influence Frau von Stein had had upon his own impassioned character. Men can be taught and restrained by noble women alone; there is no passion so unruly and no crime they might commit so utterly unforgivable, that the love, the kindness, the prayer of a fine woman cannot help them atone for it. To two women more than to anybody else Faust owed whatever he learned and was: his relationship with Margaret taught this restlessly ambitious individualist and egotist the meaning of love, of unselfishness, of sacrifice and inner peace, and his mating with Helen of Troy, the symbol of Greek Classicism, perfected the aesthetic education of this prototype of German

Romanticism as nothing else did. And when Faust came to die and the hosts of the Lord and of Satan were struggling for his possession, it was the spirit of Margaret that descended and interceded in his behalf, leading him heavenwards and pleading for him before God. Dante, whose ascent to heaven in the company of Beatrice had served as Goethe's model, had concluded his mighty epic by glorifying the love of God which moves Heaven and all the other stars; Goethe, however, the intense lover and grateful worshipper of women, concluded his mighty drama by glorifying womanhood which, in its finest qualities, will always draw man upwards, heavenwards.

For Schiller, too, the love of woman alone can ennoble and deify man and complete his aesthetic education, and, angered by the obscene sneers in Voltaire's *Maid of Orleans*, Schiller showed in his own work by the same name that the angelic figure of one woman, Joan of Arc, could indeed save not only individuals but entire nations from the chains of foreign oppressors and from the darkness, the follies and the faithlessness of their souls. In Wagner's *Tannhäuser*, after even a heartless Pope had refused to forgive the hero for his sins in Venusberg, it was again the prayer of a loving, saintly woman, Elizabeth of Thuringia, who dying achieved the miracle of Tannhäuser's salvation. Even though Friedrich Halm is a very minor figure in German literature, he should be mentioned here too, for his treatment of *Griseldis*, in the century-long history of descriptions of the humiliation of a spineless woman, for the first time depicted a proud heroine who in the name of her own dignity and self-respect refused to return home after her brutal husband had seen fit to call her back. Exquisite and appreciative analyses of fine womanly characters we find also in the dramas of Friedrich Hebbel, the great representative of nineteenth-century Realism; no wonder that in two modern novels, Gerhart Hauptmann's *The Heretic of Soana* and Richard Voss' *Two Souls*, the love and kindness of womanhood begin to make their wondrous power felt even among young priests who, in their troubled hearts, have long ago begun to doubt the validity and the ethical justification of the Catholic vow of celibacy.

The German poets' constant preoccupation with one great individual's hunger for God, for happiness, for a valid philosophy of life, has, however this one great disadvantage, that to most Germans the idea means infinitely more than the form. Perhaps some of the peculiarities of the German language encouraged this trend of presenting significant human thoughts, the result of crisis, despair and sublimation, in an involved, complicated and laborious fashion. German literature is very rarely elegant: its ponderings as well as its phrases are telescoped one into the other, cumbersome, heavy, at times exasperating. Not so French literature: it says whatever it has to say urbanely, fluently, wittily. In fact we may often wonder whether the cult of form—the sonority of the alexandrine, the fourteen lines of the sonnet, the polish of an epigram or the "esprit" of a novel—has not become so supreme in French literature that the depth of thought underneath it all has begun to suffer because of it. Here is certainly another instance where classical France and romantic Germany can ideally complement and enrich each other: whenever skilled French stylists need more food for thought than is momentarily available to them, they can turn to, and profit by, the soul-searching, irrational and mystical qualities of German literature, as Renan, Quinet, Michelet, Gide and Rolland did; and whenever German poets, wrestling with the problems and with the angels and devils that contend in them, feel the need of greater fluency, lucidity, beauty and urbanity, they can turn to and profit by the gifts of the genius of France, of Italy or of ancient Greece. Countless German poets and artists, from Gottfried von Strassburg and Albrecht Dürer through Wieland, Goethe and Platen, down to Stefan George, Thomas Mann and Ricarda Huch in our own days, have benefitted immensely by adding to their own German inheritance—the thought—the beauty and exquisiteness of form to be found in the Mediterranean countries. In fact, we might perhaps add that at least in the case of Germany a perfect masterpiece of literature or art is not possible unless, somehow, sometime, the artist has found it possible to amalgamate the German depth of thought and the French beauty of form.

These, then, are some of the German contributions to European literature. As we analyze them detachedly, we may consider some of them good, others potentially dangerous—but we cannot deny the very great significance of their impact upon Western culture. Germany, at the crossroads of all currents, open in every direction, the land of the middle, as she likes to be called, neither completely Western like France nor semi-Asian like Russia, always has been and always will be, not only the heart, but also the battleground of Europe, where new ideas meet, to clash or blend. In her finest moments she can act as the great mediator and take over the beautiful role of cultural leadership, as she did one hundred and fifty years ago when America also came under the spell of the light emanating from Weimar, Jena and Königsberg—and in her worst moments she has become a traitor to Western Civilization, opening doors and gates wide to atavistic, barbarian forces—comparable indeed to a Faust, the man of two souls, for whose possession the forces of Light and of Darkness are struggling. For obvious reasons I have not dwelled too much on these unsavory and sufficiently known aspects of the German mentality—the fanatical nationalism in Hutten and Kleist, the philosophy of Nietzsche, the exalted racial mysticism beginning, perhaps, with Hamann and leading, in the recent past, to the aberrations of the so-called Blood and Soil authors of the Third Reich, many of which, as you may have noticed, very can often be traced back to some undesirable aspect of Romanticism. Rather than hold a "post-mortem" especially over the years from 1914 to 1945, it seemed more worthwhile and constructive to point to several traits and traditions of German culture which indicate that most of it is an integral part of the general culture of the Western, the Atlantic World after all. If we cherish all the constituent elements of this Western culture—the Romania and the Germania and the Anglo-Saxon world which is deeply and equally rooted in both these cultural blocs—then we need not fear that, in the looming struggle between the East and the West, Germany will become a No Man's Land, uncertain of her allegiance, for, for the sake of what was given to us by Beethoven, Goethe, and Kant, we may yet find it thoroughly worth our while, if not imperative, to help her to be anchored safely on this side of the chasm.

If it is generally granted that the Age of Romanticism coincided with the great wave of political, social, and spiritual liberation which may be said to have lasted from the French Revolution to the idealistic aspirations of 1830 and 1848, then we certainly must admit that the last generation of German romanticists failed pitifully to keep pace with the evolving freedom of man. Instead, these late romanticists represented an inactive, if not downright reactionary, group of authors who, by their meek acceptance of the *status quo* under Metternich, betrayed the legitimate hopes of their people, and the noble visions and goals of Romanticism in general.

This political failure of the poets between 1815 and 1830 becomes all the more evident if we compare their acceptance of oppression with the militant patriotism of those other romanticists who had just preceded them, the Kleists, Fichtes, Arndts and Körners who, between 1806 and 1815, between Jena and Waterloo, had fought in the first ranks of German liberation. The political failure after 1815 becomes even more obvious if we compare the late romanticists of Germany with the great romantic authors of the rest of Europe who, almost without exception, remained loyal to the great political and revolutionary ideals of the Romantic School and who, therefore, even after 1830 and 1848, stayed on as the great battlers against oppression and as the great liberators of, and spokesmen for, their people. Not so the Germans whose will to resist and to fight ceased after 1815 — and some twenty years later it then took an entirely different group of poets with a different literary program,

[1]Lecture given in Calcutta, August, 1959 and reprinted from the *Jadavpur Journal of Comparative Literature*, I, 1961, 1-9.

the Young Germans—realists rather than romanticists, pamphleteers rather than poets—to pick up the weapons too quickly and too easily discarded by the romanticists, and to finish the fight against Metternich.

Only England, among all European nations, shared with Germany a general apathy—not right after 1815, to be sure, but at least some eight or ten years later, after Byron and Shelley, the greatest battlers and idealists, had died. But in defence of this attitude we can at least say that England was a relatively progressive, liberal country which did not share in the cruel oppression of human rights practised by the Holy Alliance on the continent, and that English literature, therefore, with the coming of the Victorians, could afford to be considerably less militant and less fiercely inspired than it had been before. But everywhere else the fight was on after 1815—a fight begun and continued by the romanticists, and finished by the romanticists (except in Germany) decades and generations later, even after other -isms had begun to appear on the scene. In France, Chateaubriand and Lamartine and the ex-Swiss Benjamin Constant became political leaders, with political roles added to their literary significance, right through the midst of the 1830 and the 1848 revolutions. Even Musset, not always a plaintive "Weltschmerz"-poet, managed to become militant and to strike back at the Young Germans' *Rheinlied*—"Sie sollen ihn nicht haben, den freien, deutschen Rhein!"—with a sarcastic and yet martial poem of his own, "Nous l'avons eu, votre Rhin allemand!" But the most indefatigable battler for freedom among the French romanticists was, of course, Victor Hugo, the author of *Les Misérables*, whose vitality and fervor carried him far beyond 1848. His main political enemy, the butt of his fiercest attacks, was Napoleon III—and even after 1871 Hugo remained an ever-ready champion of human liberty, to his very last day.

In Italy the sacred gospel of the absolute necessity of freeing the peninsula from foreign domination was so old, so strong, and so ever-present, that we can easily see traces of the "Risorgimento" as early as Dante, Machiavelli, Alfieri—and, with regard to the romanticists, naturally in Foscolo, Monti, Manzoni, in authors of patriotic historical novels like Grossi and Guerrazzi, in exiled patriots like Mazzini and Gabriele Rossetti, and in martyrs like Silvio Pellico, whose account of his incarceration by the Austrians in the notorious Spielberg, *Le mie prigioni*, became a European best-seller in the great continental struggle against the system of Metternich. I think it is rather difficult to draw the line and say where Romanticism ended and where the "Risorgimento" began, for the age of Manzoni and the later age of Carducci vied with each other in militant fervor and resiliency which again contrasted the volatile and unafraid Italians so greatly with the passively acquiescing Germans and Austrians north of them.

Greater even—to the point of the romantic poet's becoming a messiah or a martyr for his oppressed countrymen—was the militant role of the romanticists in Eastern Europe. As two of the most striking examples of this absolute devotion to the cause of freedom, I need mention only the Hungarian national poet Petöfi who, in the wake of the revolution of 1848, died on the battlefield defending his country against the Russian allies of Metternich; and the Polish national poet and romanticist, Adam Mickiewicz who, to a people kept in oppression, held up, in his great epic poem *Konrad Wallenrod*, a picture of earlier Polish valor defeating the Teutonic Knights in the fifteenth century. Mickiewicz died in 1855while engaged in the important patriotic task of recruiting in Western Europe a legion of Polish volunteers who, through their participation in the Crimean War, might contribute to the defeat of Russia and to the long overdue liberation of Poland.

Indeed, we can safely say that in the United States also some at least of the romantic poets, prose-masters and thinkers participated in the great struggle for human freedom in general and for the abolition of slavery in particular, with Bryant, Thoreau and Lowell foremost among them. Somehow it seemed natural all over the world that Romanticism and the great political and social upheavals of the first two thirds of the nineteenth century should go hand in hand.

Not so in Germany. To be sure, there was militant political poetry in Germany, too—but it was written either before 1815, like Rückert's *Geharnischte Sonette.* or by Young Germans rather than romanticists, after 1840, like Herwegh's *Gedichte eines Lebendigen.* To be sure, one can find compassionate lyrical outbursts for the oppressed and against the oppressors even in the critical period between 1815 and 1830—but such outbursts did not dare to concern themselves with German conditions. It seemed safer to speak of distant, foreign oppressions instead, as did Wilhelm Müller's *Lieder der Griechen* and Chamisso's *Lord Byrons letzte Liebe* on behalf of the Greeks in their valiant struggle against the Turks, or Platen's *Polenlieder* and Julius Mosen's *Die letzten zehn vom vierten Regiment* on behalf of the cruelly oppressed Polish victims of Russian brutality. But otherwise the vast bulk of late romantic literature in Germany does not dare to concern itself with the scandalous political situation at home. To be sure, there were protests, incarcerations, banishments among the German authors who dared to speak up; but these men, I repeat, were not romanticists, but were Young Germans or realists: Laube and Reuter who were imprisoned at home, Heine and Börne who went to France, Freiligrath to England, Herwegh to Switzerland. The late romantic writers of Germany, instead, escaped into nonpolitical realms of poetic imagination: Eichendorff and Lenau sang of the beauties of nature as they had rarely been sung before (unless their frequent preoccupation with autumn and dying indicated a slightly subversive subtlety), while E.T.A. Hoffmann (to mention just one more typical late romanticist) with his *Fantasiestücke* and his *Nachtstücke* escaped into the politically equally harmless realm of stark fantasy and grotesque weirdness.

In their enormous influence abroad, great Germans before 1815 had given political and cultural pride and virility to downtrodden nations. Thus Herder's enormous impact upon the racial awakening and awareness of the Slavic peoples of Eastern Europe; thus also the amazingly uplifting influence of the two Schlegels upon Italy, Spain and Portugal, when these famous critics, in spite of the past enmity and scorn of classical France, declared Dante, Camoens and Lope de Vega to be every inch as great as, if not much greater than, the much vaunted so-called best authors of classical France. But this same invigoration did not last in the case of the Germans — and whatever virility and strength and pride in past cultural greatness they had shown in their fight against Napoleon (Kleist, Fichte, Görres, Arnim, Brentano, the Grimm brothers), seemed mostly to desert them when Metternich's system undid the hoped-for fruits of Waterloo. Search as I may, I can find only one lone romanticist who, by 1848, felt still young and idealistic enough to participate in the deliberations of the National Assembly in Frankfurt: it was Ludwig Uhland.

In recent decades, as if because of awareness that such an attitude of utter passivity, not to say defeatism, should not be connected with the bold and challenging term Romanticism at all, a new term has been created in order to designate that atmosphere of unheroic living, of small bourgeois contentment, of lack of resilience and rebellion in the face of a tyranny imposed from above: "Biedermeier." If that term, borrowed from the art of Ludwig Richter and Karl Spitzweg, were to be accepted, we would apply it especially to men like Grillparzer in order to indicate the frustration of life in the very den of the lion, the Vienna of Metternich. Perhaps we could extend the validity of this term "Biedermeier" beyond the two dates set by us, 1815 and 1830, and we might include as an earlier representative Jean Paul, whose *Schulmeisterlein Wuz* and *Quintus Fixlein* were quite harmless little fellows indeed, dreamers rather than doers, completely unpolitical and unheroic at any rate. And, going beyond 1830, we might include the passive, frustrated life of Mörike; indeed, we might perhaps go as far as Stifter. Significantly enough, the term "Biedermeier" does not seem to fit in at all with other literatures, which again seems to indicate that this passivity of late German Romanticism is quite unique in Western literature—and one cannot think of a French of Italian "Biedermeier" author, and perhaps only in England could we find similar representatives of repressed life as, for instance, in the Brontës and the heroines of their novels.

But, no doubt, this complete passivity of the typical "Biedermeier" is particularly strikingly represented by Grillparzer, and I should like to mention three of his dramas to illustrate this point: *Der Bruderzwist in Habsburg, Der Traum ein Leben,* and *Ein treuer Diener seines Herrn.* The first two dramas are easily characterized by the deeply symbolical perversion of Schiller's famous line, "Der Übel grösstes ist die Schuld" —for in the late romantic "Biedermeier" Grillparzer this line now significantly reads "Der Übel grösstes ist die Tat": the greatest of all evils is man's positive deed, a deed which may so easily be or become arrogant or criminal or at variance with God's inscrutable will.

In *The Brotherly Feud in Habsburg*, Grillparzer shows us an early seventeenth-century emperor, Rudolf II, for whom all action seems blasphemous presumptuousness, because man in his blindness and ignorance time and again is apt to upset the God-ordained delicate equilibrium of the Universe. Persevering, passive persevering and enduring seem to be the only philosophy of life for this Habsburg emperor on the eve of the Thirty Years' War which he tried to avoid through his own complete passivity, just as it was the only philosophy of life for the late romantic poets fearful of Metternich's repressive powers:

> Es gibt Lagen, wo ein Schritt voraus
> Und einer rückwärts gleicherweis verderblich.
> Da hält man sich denn ruhig, und erwartet
> Bis frei der Weg, den Gott dem Rechten ebnet.

Or again:

> Fragst aber du: ob sie mir selber kund,
> Die hohe Wahrheit aus der Wesen Munde?
> So sag' ich: nein, und aber wieder: nein.
> Ich bin ein schwacher, unbegabter Mann.
> Der Dinge tiefster Kern ist mir verschlossen.
> Doch ward mir Fleiss und noch ein andres: Ehrfurcht
> Für das, dass andre mächtig und ich nicht.

And finally:

> Ich bin das Band, das diese Garbe hält,
> Unfruchtbar selbst, doch nötig, weil es bindet.

These are words of utter submissiveness which, if spoken by, and true for a ruler, Rudolf II, surely are, or should be, even more valid for the humble subject who is even more ignorant of the unfathomable will of the stars and of their creator.

And if man feels that he simply must act and rebel, then, Grillparzer teaches us in his *The Dream A Life*, let him at least act and sin and become guilty and punishable only in his dreams, and not in his waking hours. And so Rustan (sometimes called the Austrian Faust, and sarcastically so,

131

because the German Faust strives and achieves in full reality, while Grillparzer's hero only dreams that he does so) is more than relieved when at the end of his long nightmare he realizes that his ambitious schemes and his concomitant guilt and punishment have not been real, after all, but only a bad dream—and that in real life he is still harmless and innocent:

> Breit' es aus mit deinen Strahlen,
> Senk' es tief in jede Brust:
> Eines nur ist Glück hienieden,
> Eins: des Innern stiller Frieden
> Und die schuldbefreite Brust!
> Und die Grösse ist gefährlich,
> Und der Ruhm ein leeres Spiel;
> Was er gibt, sind nicht'ge Schatten,
> Was er nimmt, es ist so viel!

In the third and last drama to be mentioned, *A Loyal Servant of His Master*, I am naturally aware of the fact that a very strong and favorable case can be made for Bancbanus, too—a man so utterly loyal to his temporarily absent ruler, King Andreas of Hungary, who had enjoined him to keep strictest order in the realm while he himself was gone, that he did not arrest and punish the villain, the queen's brother, who through his viciousness had driven Bancbanus' own young wife into despair and suicide. Still, in spite of Bancbanus' unquestioning loyalty to his pledged word to preserve the peace of the land, one cannot help looking on him, too, as a depressing example of complete servility, as a man who completely disregards his own personal sufferings and claims to revenge for the sake of a so-called higher cause, peace within the kingdom. And even when the embittered Hungarians start a rebellion against the queen and her despicable brother, Bancbanus refuses to side with them; instead, he fights them, his own friends, relatives and supporters, for the king alone has the right to punish, and Bancbanus has a blind faith that the king will surely do that after he has returned. And, a still more striking example of the suppression of his own grievances, when the rebels invade the royal castle, Bancbanus saves not only the queen and the young prince, but also the queen's brother, the fiend who has caused the pathetic death of Bancbanus' wife. One is reminded of the rather notorious Prussian political motto of "Ordnung ist die erste Bürgerpflicht" as this prototype of a loyal, self-effacing servant and subject of the king exclaims:

> Es wird sich weisen, kehrt der König wieder,
> Und das soll bald, gemeldet ward's ihm schon.
> Der nun wird sitzen mit dem Schwert des Rechts,
> Wer rein, wer schuldig, wird sein Wort entscheiden.
> Bis dahin haltet euch als ruh'ge Bürger.

And again:

> Ich bin der Nächste, dem man sie geraubt,
> Dem man sein Heil, dem man sein Glück getötet,
> Mein Kind, mein Weib, mein Alles auf der Welt.
> Wenn nun nicht ich, wer ist so kühn und redet?

These, then, are a few amazing examples of the kind of mentality that pervaded the late German romanticists. Why this should be so, why in their spinelessness they differed so greatly from all those other late European romanticists, the Hugos, the Petöfis, the Mickiewiczes, who kept on battling until victory was achieved, is hard to tell. I can offer only a few suggestions. One might be that a certain German vice, the lack of civic courage, the inborn unwillingness to oppose the dictates of men in uniform, though prevalent throughout the ages, achieved its worst moments in that period between 1815 and 1830. Or again I might refer to the strange German predilection for calling themselves a nation of Hamlets — at a time when the First Reich was dead and the Second Reich not yet born, and when the hesitant burghers oscillated, not knowing whether they should first strive for imperial reunification at the one extreme, or for true democratic freedom at the other — and, not knowing, they drifted along like Hamlet, dreaming rather than doing. Other reasons for this passivity in the face of Metternich's Holy Alliance were, of course, the two facts that an amazing number of German romanticists were aristocrats by birth, and that, furthermore, an equally amazing number were Catholics in their religious affiliation

—which, again, at least in part, explains an ultra-conservative outlook and an evident unwillingness to storm the barricades.

At the end of the long Napoleonic Wars in which Goethe had refused to participate and from which he had proudly held aloof like an Olympian god, he had been capable of condemning his previous aloofness, of apologizing to his contemporaries, and of vowing that henceforth he would take a real and immediate interest in all political and social problems of his fellow-Germans—and so he had written, in his *Des Epimenides Erwachen* of 1814, the truly great lines of

> Doch schäm' ich mich der Ruhestunden,
> Mit Euch zu leiden wär' Gewinn,
> Denn für den Schmerz, den Ihr empfunden,
> Seid Ihr auch grösser als ich bin.

But, alas, around 1830, we look in vain for a similar confession of guilt, a similar admission of blindness and indifference, from the late-romantic poets of Germany as they watched their fellow-countymen, the students, the burghers, the Young Germans, rise up against oppression. They could not do what, perhaps, they were not meant to do.

XII. THE CHANGING ATTITUDE OF AMERICAN AUTHORS TOWARDS EUROPE[1]

This brief discussion of the great literary and cultural give-and-take that occurs between Europe and America and of the changing attitude of American authors towards European culture and literature will be made clearer if we subdivide the entire period of American letters into four different phases, of which the first two, from 1620 to 1860, were entirely subservient to the standards and values emanating from Europe, while the third phase, from 1860 to about 1890, strove for a complete spiritual independence from, and rejection of, the European pattern. It is only in the fourth and last phase, since about 1900, that a fairly equitable coexistence has been achieved, with the American authors willing to live and let live, to give to and to absorb from Europe, almost entirely without those excessively pro-European or anti-European complexes which are apt to mar many inherently fine efforts in formerly colonial literatures.

The first phase, the colonial literature from the middle of the seventeenth century to the end of the eighteenth, did not especially distinguish itself by its literary qualities, for neither the Puritans around 1650 nor the battlers for freedom from the political oppression of George III around 1775 were excessively given to aesthetic considerations. Still, what literary influences there were, were almost exclusively English—John Milton and Alexander Pope foremost among them—though it should be emphasized, too, that the religious and political impact of Europe was far stronger than whatever echoes European literature evoked in colo-

[1]Address delivered at the Plenary Session of the Australasian Universities' Modern Language Association Congress in Brisbane, August 1955, and reprinted from AUMLA, May 1956, 15-29.

nial America. In religion, of course, the impact of English Puritanism was supreme – to which can be added various Protestant contributions from Germany, Switzerland and France: Luther, Zwingli, Calvin, du Bartas, though these continental influences were always distinctly secondary to the overwhelming influence of the English mother-country upon the young, struggling colonies. Outstanding among the great Puritan absorbers of the heritage of English Protestantism was Increase Mather, a theologian, pamphleteer, political and religious leader and teacher rather than a distinctly literary figure. He was of importance not only as the absolutistic head of the Boston theocracy, but also as a statesman in the wider sense of the word because, after the downfall of Puritanism in England and the restoration of the Stuarts, it was he who became the first unofficial political and cultural ambassador of his fellow-Americans in London and who, while safeguarding colonial and Puritan interests, had to carry out the very difficult task of negotiating a new *modus vivendi* with an inherently anti-Puritan and anti-democratic Charles II and James II. A more distinctly literary link in this Puritan age not much given to *belles-lettres* can be seen in the emulation of the sternly Huguenot poetry of du Bartas and his *La première semaine ou la création du monde* by the first poetess of America, Mrs. Anne Bradstreet from Boston, whose religious and meditative poems appeared first in England in 1659 under the delightful pen-name of "The tenth Muse, lately sprung up in America."

It was only after 1750, when political considerations in the coming war against England loomed far greater than the religious exaltation of the New England Puritans, that the English hegemony as almost the sole cultural provider of America was challenged for the first time, for political enlightenment against the tyranny of kings meant, above all, the influence of France, of the enlighteners around Montesquieu and Voltaire, and also the impact of Swiss republicanism as exemplified in Rousseau's glorification, in *Le contrat social*, of the old democratic freedoms of his native Geneva. Perhaps we can afford to mention by name three or four instances of such political rather than purely literary indebtedness. Montesquieu's *Esprit des lois* of 1748 appealed especially to the rebellious colonials, inasmuch as it contained a masterful analysis of those old English freedoms which the increasingly odious George III was trying to pervert in America—and in the pre-war stages of the American Revolution Montesquieu's book therefore set up an ideal goal, a programmatic discussion of the very freedoms to which the restless colonials wanted to revert.

Benjamin Franklin—almost a hundred years after Increase Mather —the second great emissary of America to explain and to safeguard the colonial interests in London, left England for Paris after the outbreak of the actual fighting, not only because France was to be won over as a badly-needed ally in the war against England, but also because Paris was the great home of European Enlightenment, the city where Franklin met Voltaire, Turgot, Buffon and Lafayette, where he absorbed and digested the new ideas of *liberté, égalité* and *fraternité* and passed them on to his native America—for what had been a challenging topic of radical discussions and elegant *causeries* in the salons of Paris now became a bloody reality at Valley Forge and Yorktown. Another instance of the very great and real contribution of French Enlightenment to the political thinking of the young American republic is its influence upon Thomas Jefferson, the formulator of the American Declaration of Independence and the spiritual father of the modern Democratic Party, who followed Benjamin Franklin as the second American minister to France. Jefferson was in the very midst of the spiritual fermentation of the 1780's and the later outbreak of the French Revolution before, deeply imbued with the imperishable ideals of 1789, he returned to his native country to serve in the cabinet of the first President, George Washington, and later to become President himself.

It should be noted, too, that the first accurate and warm-hearted account of the new American republic, its steadily advancing Western Frontier and its tremendous future potentialities, was written by a very pro-American Frenchman, St. Jean de Crèvecoeur, who spent a few years as a farmer in the Central States before he became French consul in New York: this was his *Letters from an American Farmer* of 1782 which went through many European translations and editions and served as the most informative handbook for potential European emigrants before another Frenchman, Count Alexis de Tocqueville, superseded it in 1835 with his basically significant *De la démocratie en Amérique*. And finally, to turn to the more distinctly literary rather than political aspects of the French impact: it should also be borne in mind that Philip Freneau, sometimes called the father of American lyrical poetry, was of French extraction and that, halfway between Enlightenment and Romanticism, he always staunchly represented the ideals and traditions of France, even though the reverberations of the Napoleonic Wars and of the blockade of Europe did not always make it easy for him to serve as a self-appointed intermediary between his old native country and his new adopted one.

The second phase comprises the years from 1800 to 1860, the New York authors like Wahington Irving, James Fenimore Cooper, William Cullen Bryant and Hermann Melville, Southerners like Edgar Allan Poe and William Gilmore Simms, and especially the Golden Age of New England culture and Romanticism, of Emerson, Thoreau, Margaret Fuller, Hawthorne, Longfellow and Holmes. It was a phase in which the influence of Europe upon American literature became supreme, though religious and political currents across the Atlantic Ocean (e.g. the impact of the tenets of the French Revolution or the theology of Schleiermacher upon the Transcendentalists) remained important, if secondary, factors in American cultural life. It was a phase, too, during which the position of England as the foremost contributor to American culture was plainly weakened, for with the achievement of political independence in the thirteen former colonies, the road was free for other great cultures to make their influences felt – though, of course, this continuing closeness to English literature is not our chief concern here. Switzerland's Rousseau and Pestalozzi, and France's Saint-Simon and Fourier inspired the best utopian thinkers and planners of America whose work extended from Brook Farm in Boston to New Harmony in Indiana and beyond; and the philosophical wisdom of Plato's Greece and the mysticism of ancient India provided the foundation for the noblest programs and visions of the New England Transcendentalists.

But greatest of all was the impact of Germany, whose own culture, in the decades of Goethe, Kant and Beethoven, had at last reached its finest peak – and this influence of the Golden Age of Germany upon the

Western World in general and upon America in particular was so great that it cannot even be outlined here. It is quite significant, too, that the close intellectual bonds which still existed between England and America often served to further these German influences, too—for, with regard to the two most famous Anglo-American friendships of that time, the one between Sir Walter Scott and Washington Irving, and the other between Thomas Carlyle and Ralph Waldo Emerson, it should be borne in mind that both Englishmen were outstanding Germanophiles, Sir Walter Scott the translator of Bürger's *Leonore* and of Goethe's *Götz von Berlichingen*, Carlyle the translator and emulator of Goethe's *Wilhelm Meister* and the author of a *Life of Frederick the Great*—and in both cases, Irving and Emerson in America owed very much of their German background to their English friends.

Right after the end of the Napoleonic Wars, the American traveller became a frequent visitor in Europe; he came no longer as an argumentative priest like Increase Mather in the seventeenth century, nor as a wily diplomat like Benjamin Franklin in the eighteenth, but as a culture-seeking gentleman, a visitor to London and Paris, a student at German universities, a profound lover of Italy or of Spain. Irving was enthralled by Moorish Granada, while Longfellow visited Scandinavia, and emulated the Finnish *Kalevala* in his own *Hiawatha*; Margaret Fuller married an Italian aristocrat and took a burning interest in the "Risorgimento" of the hapless Italian peninsula, while Cooper, hard to please either at home or abroad, was most favorably impressed by the democratic institutions of Switzerland; the historian George Bancroft became a classmate of Bismarck's at Göttingen, while Lowell achieved the high honor of becoming United States ambassador to England. New cultural bonds between Europe and America were woven unceasingly, for in view of her political independence and the mighty wave of non-Anglo-Saxon immigration which was to enrich her so tremendously, America was now free to seek out and to emulate the best that was in the cultures of the northern, as well as of the Mediterranean, world. In nine cases out of ten, Europe was the giver rather than the receiver of cultural values, for the American intelligentsia, ensconced along the shores of the Atlantic Ocean, could maintain and strengthen its precarious position in the face of the barbarian prowess, conquest, expansion, materialism, greed and violence of the Middle West only by constantly dipping into the invigorating and reassuring cultural reservoir of Europe that was at its disposal. Hence now the tremendous impact of the Golden Age of German literature and philosophy which extended from Ticknor's translation of Goethe's *Werther* in 1814 to the so-called St. Louis Hegelians around 1860; the influence of Rousseau, who found the most literal-minded emulator of his return-to-nature message in Henry David Thoreau, the sage of Walden Pond near Concord, Massachusetts; the fascinating popularity of the novels of Sir Walter Scott in the pre-Civil War South, where his re-creations of medieval English chivalry may well be said to have helped to condition the entire semi-feudal way of life of the aristocratic plantation owners of Virginia and the Carolinas.

Scores of volumes have been written about the intensity of these American literary relations with Germany, England and France during the first half of the nineteenth century — and I should like to point to two other nations, whose contributions to American culture are not as well known, or as thoroughly explored: Italy and Spain. Italian awareness of the message of freedom preached by the successful American War of Liberation against England began when, in 1781, Alfieri wrote five odes *All' America libera*, and when he dedicated his *Brutus* to George Washington, that other great enemy of tyranny; while Carlo Botta, a few years later, sought to encourage a nation striving for similar liberation from foreign oppression by writing a *Storia della guerra dell' indipendenza degli Stati Uniti d'America*. Quite important as the first unofficial cultural ambassador of Italy in America was Lorenzo da Ponte, not only well known, while he was still in Europe, as the libretto-writer of Mozart's operas *Don Giovanni* and *Cosi fan tutte*, but after his arrival in America a busy little intermediary, who in essays, pamphlets, lectures and classes made Americans aware of the beauty of the Italian language and the wealth of Italian literature.

Of all the great Italian masters, Dante Alighieri was the one who always impressed the best American poets and thinkers most deeply, from about 1830 to our own days of Ezra Pound and T.S. Eliot; and rather than dwell on the fragmentary translations of the *Divina Commedia* by Parsons, the *Ugolino*-tragedy by Featherstonehaugh or the *Francesca da Rimini*-tragedy by Boker, we should stress the real mile-stones of American Dantism: Emerson's translation of the *Vita Nuova* of 1842 (the first English translation ever made, first published in Chapel Hill in 1960), Lowell's beautiful essay on Dante, Longfellow's imposing translation of the entire *Divina Commedia*, published in 1865, on the occasion of the six-hundredth anniversary of Dante's birth, and the subsequent founding of the Dante Society of America (the third in the world, after those of Italy and Germany), and Charles Eliot Norton's new prose translations of *La Vita Nuova* and *La Divina Commedia* in 1867 and 1892 respectively. The comparatist interested in the international acclaim of Dante's literary works and high ethical ideals need not wonder why these New Englanders and Harvard scholars should have been so powerfully attracted to the greatest Italian poet, for far more important than the differences between them—Dante so medieval, so Catholic, so Italian, and the Bostonians so modern and progressive, so Protestant and American—were the similarities of their philosophies of life, disciplined, austere, scholarly, God-permeated, of an ethical idealism unmatched even by Shakespeare or Goethe.

As to America's indebtedness to Spain: rather than speak of intermediaries, translations or emulations of specific Spanish works, we might choose another mode of investigation customary among comparatists, and point to Spanish history and culture as a whole, as they impressed the visiting American travellers, poets, historians and diplomats. The panorama of this Spanish influence became all the wider, because one could include also the exotic and oriental world of Spanish-Moorish relations and then, nearer home in America, the leading role of Spain in the discovery and colonization of Central and South America—two themes, in addition to the study of Spain itself, which for the sake of their rich colorfulness and breathtaking romanticism appealed greatly to the thin crust of intellectual leaders of a young nation busily engaged in the prosaic and soul-killing task of establishing a new civilization in far more inhospitable northern climes.

George Ticknor, the first important American traveller in Spain and later the first teacher of Modern Languages at Harvard, is remembered to this very day for his often reprinted and basically important *History of Spanish Literature*. He was followed by Washington Irving, one of the most cultured and discriminating American visitors in Europe and later American ambassador to Spain, whose years on the Iberian Peninsula inspired books like his immortal *Alhambra* (1832), his *Chronicle of the Conquest of Granada* and his *Legends of the Conquest of Spain*, and marginal works like his *Mahomet and his Successors* on the one hand, and his *History of the Life of Columbus* and the *Voyages of the Companions of Columbus* on the other. Rather than point to Spanish elements in Poe or Longfellow, we might add that the historian William Hickling Prescott then continued the work begun by Washington Irving, writing either about Spain itself (his *History of Ferdinand and Isabella* of 1837 and his unfinished *History of Philip II*) or then about the hispanization and christianization of Spanish America (his *History of the Conquest of Mexico* of 1843 and his *Conquest of Peru*).

These hints about the cultural impact of Italy and Spain must suffice; many other interesting ties with Europe (Chateaubriand's very controversial *Voyage en Amérique*, Goethe's interesting remarks and hopes concerning America as expressed in his *Wilhelm Meisters Wanderjahre*, Lenau's heartbreaking experiences in Ohio, etc.) cannot be more than alluded to here. One thing, though, must still be stated before we conclude with this second phase of American-European literary relations: that two American authors began to influence Europe in their turn; one, not very good, James Fenimore Cooper, because he had the good luck to be the first to stumble across the very rich and appealing topic of the American Indian which, from his *Leatherstocking Tales* on, swept like wildfire all over Europe; and the other, Edgar Allan Poe, for the two reasons that his exquisite art appealed greatly to the later Parnassians and Symbolists of Europe and that the genre perfected by him, often called the detective story, or ratiocinative tale, was destined to become immensely popular in the twentieth century. With the endless translations of Cooper and the popularity of the new Red Indian themes, the ground was also prepared for a German translation of Longfellow's *Hiawatha* by Freiligrath in 1857 — and among the German emulators of Cooper's Western background should be named especially the Austrian

Karl Postl, whose American tales, published under the name of Charles Sealsfield, achieved a broad popular success. As to the far greater artistic achievement of Edgar Allan Poe: Baudelaire's translation of his tales in 1856 and Mallarmé's French version of *The Raven* and other poems in 1888 made him a first-class literary power in Europe, and his impact, in both style and content, was early and lasting, from Gautier, Verlaine and Rimbaud in the West to Dostoevsky in the East.

After this period of greatest admiration for Europe's cultural values by American authors, as indicated in its wide range by Bryant's translation of Homer's *Iliad* and *Odyssey* and Bayard Taylor's rendering of Goethe's *Faust*, it seemed natural that in a new phase, our third phase, the pendulum should swing to the other extreme and that, with Walt Whitman, there should begin a period of emphatic anti-Europeanism. The roots of this all-American attitude can be traced as far back as George Washington's *Farewell Address* of 1797, when the first President of the United States besought his countrymen to have as little to do with the affairs of Europe as possible—or as the Monroe Doctrine of 1823, which forbade European interventions in American problems. But these declarations had been political and economic rather than literary; they were the expression of the will of the new millions of immigrants in the Middle West who had been unhappy and miserable in strife-torn old Europe and who henceforth wanted to place as wide a chasm as they could between the Old World and the New. Culturally, however, the influence of Europe continued unabated through the decades of Irving and Longfellow, and it was only from the Civil War on that this European leadership was first doubted and then deflated.

With the holocaust of the Civil War, America at last began to discover her own self and her own titanic strength and variety, the folklores of the North and the South and the West, the dominating role of the ever-advancing American Frontier in the shaping of the American character, the hills of Vermont, the cotton of Georgia, the lakes of Minnesota, the plains of Kansas, the mountains of Colorado, the life on the Mississippi, the soul of the Negro, the homespun humor of the pioneers, the gold of California. Here was a whole new continent ready to be exploited, economically as well as poetically. The most urgent literary need of the day seemed to be the creation of a great all-American epic (a hope unfulfilled to this very day) which would sing of the mountains and the prairies, the white, the red and the black inhabitants of America, of the cities and the rivers and the forests, of the New Yorkers and the Texans, of the vices and the virtues of that grand and overflowing melting-pot which is America—and, failing in that great aspiration to write an epic of the conquest of the West which would equal the deeds of valor immortalized by Homer, Virgil, Camoens or Tasso, one could at least write fragments of that epic as Walt Whitman did in his epoch-making *Leaves of Grass* of 1855, and as the regional novelists tried to do in the scores of works written between 1865 and 1900. To be sure, Emerson had been the first to visualize the possibility of a new exclusively American literature which would dare to disregard the European patterns and fashions—but it was only Walt Whitman who made that vision come true, who dared to be grandiosely and boisterously his own self, tall, fleshy, hairy, arrogant, titanic, a superman, a Tarzan among the effete epigones around him. It was not that Whitman was more anti-European than the average American around 1870, who considered the United States as God's own country and who had a concept of Europe as the very lair of medieval barbarity and injustice; it was simply that he ignored Europe, that in his life as well as in his poetry, in form as well as in content, he simply did not need the European or any other foreign model. After the declaration of political independence in 1776, there now came the declaration of a spiritual independence from Europe—and after Whitman we see that same proud Americanism and colorful regionalism in the poetry, and especially in the prose, of many new authors, ranging from Sidney Lanier in Georgia to Joaquin Miller in Nevada, from the old Louisiana of George Washington Cable to the Indiana of Edward Eggleston, from Mark Twain in Missouri to Bret Harte in California, indeed, somewhat later, to Jack London in Alaska and back again to the earthy Frontier-humorists like Josh Billings and Artemus Ward.

For most of these men, the importance of Europe had sunk to a minimum—in fact, in Mark Twain, more than in any other American, we notice a more bitterly anti-European and especially anti-English prejudice than is encountered in any American author before 1870. To be sure, Mark Twain, like Bret Harte, had gone to Europe on extensive travels and lecture-trips, just as Charles Dickens and Thackeray had gone to America—and though he was lionized in Paris and Berlin and even in London, and hailed as the first true American and was an immense success with his quaint drawl and his flair for humor, Mark Twain never quite saw eye to eye with Europe, and he preferred a progressive American civilization of telephones and bathtubs to all the medieval castles and social prejudices of England. In his *Innocents Abroad* and *A Tramp Abroad*, he expressed himself with Gargantuan but good-natured banter about the many shortcomings of Europe—but he reserved his greatest venom for more serious books like *The Prince and the Pauper* and *A Connecticut Yankee at the Court of King Arthur*. For these two books, far more than mere children's stories, represent a wholesale condemnation of a merry old England which in truth had never been merry at all, since the age of chivalry and of the Renaissance in Europe in general, and in England in particular, had always been full of brutality, torture, misery and starvation, with endless wars, atavistic legislation and social discrimination making the life of the common people all but unbearable. It is of course easy to accuse Mark Twain of prejudice, of an unwillingness to acknowledge that, with greater liberty and decency in the treatment of men, life had considerably changed for the better between the ages of King Arthur and of Queen Victoria, in England as well as on the Continent—but that is the way Mark Twain chose to look at Europe, as perhaps a picturesque, but certainly also a barbarian, backward and decadent group of nations to which forward-forging America, the land of the free, the Utopia of tomorrow, should no longer be exposed. Also Mark Twain's *Life of Joan of Arc*, in many respects perhaps his finest book, represents medieval Europe (and Europe will always be medieval for men like him) as a Continent full of hatred, superstition and fanaticism, of an ignorance and blackness all the blacker if contrasted with Joan of Arc, the one figure of light and hope and faith and decency who, however, had to be burnt at the stake because she was too good, too humane and far advanced for that kind of Europe.

After these two extreme oscillations of the pendulum—the admiration and emulation of Europe around 1830 and the rejection of Europe around 1880 or, to put it in other terms, the glorification of the Spanish Middle Ages by Washington Irving and of the Italian and German Middle Ages by Longfellow, followed by the no less emphatic scorn of these Middle Ages by Walt Whitman and Mark Twain—we now come to the fourth and last phase. Roughly speaking, it set in in 1900 and it finally brought peace and mutual tolerance. To be sure, the seismographic needle but rarely stands in a completely neutral position of passive co-existence and more or less pronounced indifference, for around 1900 the American naturalists again borrowed from Europe while, in the 1930's, Europe began to borrow from America. But at least they have learned to accept each other, to face each other as almost equal partners, to live and to let live.

American authors in particular have learned to get rid of an inferiority complex that is apt to haunt any colonial or ex-colonial country, to stand firmly and proudly on their own feet, to stop worrying excessively about the criticism or the applause of European arbiters of taste, book-reviewers and publishers—while on the other hand they have also got rid of their short-sighted isolationism and their more often than not arrogant nationalism, and have come to acknowledge the common cultural inheritance of the two continents and the common bond that will forever unite America and Europe. Every nation—in literature as well as in all other matters—has to learn to stop being either excessively apologetic and self-debasing or excessively aggressive and self-inflating—and for America that moment of achieving an inner balance and of acknowledging a common humaneness with the Western World came well before 1914. Even in the very midst of Mark Twain's All-Americanism, calmer realists and finer artists like William Dean Howells and Henry James had preserved an abiding love for Italy, Howells as U.S. consul in Italy (like Hawthorne before him), James in novels dealing with expatriate Americans in Italy like *Daisy Miller* and *Roderick Hudson*. With the coming of Naturalism, of course, American authors were inevitably drawn into the orbit of the great novelists of France and Russia and of the Marxist concepts emanating from Germany—and the influence of a single Frenchman, Emile Zola, can clearly be discerned in Frank Norris, Theodore Dreiser, Upton Sinclair, up to our own days of John Dos Passos and James T. Farrell, while Guy de Maupassant found a very earnest emulator in O. Henry. It would certainly lead too far to trace also the various contributions of Russia or Scandinavia in American Naturalism—but we can point to Jack London as a fascinating example of multiple foreign influences which he may not always have been able to co-ordinate properly, for besides the standard patterns of Naturalism his novels also reveal the very great influence of Darwin, Marx and Nietzsche. And a generation after this European-inspired first period of Naturalism, there came the second period of Naturalism between the two World Wars, in which American authors were givers rather than receivers in the concert of modern literatures, as the international popularity of American novelists like Hemingway and Steinbeck seems to indicate. The new leading role of America as an emittor of values is also indicated by the fact that in recent years she has received an amazing number of Nobel prizes—Sinclair Lewis, Eugene O'Neill and William Faulkner, for instance.

This peaceful new co-existence of the literatures of the two continents, this shedding of outgrown ideas about being superior or inferior to one another, this mutual permeation with literary influences gracefully given and, in most cases, gracefully received, is illustrated also by various new developments which deserve mention. In the field of lyrical poetry, both the Parnassians and the Symbolists of France have influenced an international brotherhood of poets where it is often difficult to draw national lines. Especially the Anglo-American imitators of Gautier and Baudelaire and then again of Verlaine, Mallarmé and Rimbaud are so closely interrelated, that they are usually referred to as the Anglo-American poets or Imagists, as though the barrier of the Atlantic Ocean did not exist. The best symbol of the essential oneness of poets like Ezra Pound, Eliot, Yeats, Auden, MacLeish, Williams or Hart Crane is the fact that the Englishman Auden emigrated to America, while the American T.S. Eliot (following in the footsteps of the American novelist Henry James) emigrated to England. Other young American poets of this group, like Julian Green, Stuart Merrill and

147

Francis Vielé-Griffin, preferred to live and write in France, the center of the movement, while Ezra Pound, another expatriate American, felt most at home in the Italy of Gabriele d'Annunzio. Of course, the United States had known expatriates before, cultured patricians or millionaires and their descendants who preferred to live in London, Paris, Rome or Baden-Baden (and no American author had been more acrimonious in his attacks upon spineless expatriates who were ashamed of Pittsburgh, Milwaukee or Kalamazoo than Mark Twain in his *Innocents Abroad*), but this emigration of writers like James and Eliot, Stuart Merrill and Ezra Pound (and among our modern novelists, of Ernest Hemingway and Richard Wright) now involved significant literary figures whose temporary or permanent abode abroad need not necessarily be interpreted as an anti-American gesture. Instead, they may have realized, much sooner than the American politicians and the dwindling isolationists of the Middle West, the basic unity of Western culture, the irresistible, continuing amalgamation of Europe and America which makes these two continents the very bulwark of the Western way of life and which also makes the actual seat of residence of an author relatively unimportant.

Other factors tend to build bridges between the two continents—I need refer only to the flood of German authors—liberals, pacifists, socialists and others—who in the 1930's made New York and California the headquarters for German literature in exile: Mann, Zweig, Werfel, Toller, Döblin, Remarque, Feuchtwanger, Brecht and others, who derived new strength and new resilience from their stay in a country that was so eager to welcome them and to absorb their cultural contributions. Many American authors have also begun to deal most sympathetically with the problems and the heartaches of European immigrants as they try to adjust themselves to the American way of life —for instance, Willa Cather with her beautiful novel *My Antonia* which deals with a Bohemian girl in the Middle West, or d'Agostino with his *Olives in the Apple Tree* about the tragedies and the comedies of Italian immigrants. Nothing characterizes better the tremendous advantages of the American melting-pot, the breaking down of a narrowly Anglo-Saxon pattern and its permeation with a dozen rich and old cultural traditions of the Old World, amalgamating all of them into something which is new and fascinating and strikingly American, than the racial background of some of modern America's leading authors and critics — for there are the German background in Theodore Dreiser, the Portuguese ancestry of John Dos Passos, the Italian aspects in Frances Winwar and Bernard De Voto, the Armenian contribution in William Saroyan, the Jewish element in Sholem Asch and, last but most certainly not least the Negro problem in Langston Hughes, Richard Wright and James Baldwin.

I should like to conclude by referring briefly to two modern American novels which deal with this unceasing and important groping for an acceptable *modus vivendi* between the United States and Europe — one, *Dodsworth* by Sinclair Lewis, showing the tragic and seemingly unbridgeable cleavage between the two worlds, while the other, *The Plutocrat* by Booth Tarkington, points the way to a better understanding and a happier solution.

In *Dodsworth*, the story of an American self-made man and millionaire, it was the wife who felt attracted to the social splendor of Europe and who finally persuaded her husband to accompany her on a grand tour of European capitals, where she was immediately and entirely absorbed by the glittering life among aristocrats, gamblers and gigolos. The book may be the tragedy of an aging and restless woman who is ashamed of her country and bored with her good husband, and who prefers the tinsel of Monte Carlo to such an extent that she finally asks for a divorce — but here we are concerned more with Dodsworth himself, the American abroad, strong, self-reliant, proud of his America, of his factories, of his success in life, of his ability to contribute to the civilization and therefore to the comfort of his fellowmen, instinctively aware of the fact that he is more of a man and a builder than all these "fourflushers" and phrase-makers with monocles and spats in the *salons* and the casinos of Europe. Theirs were two entirely different worlds, and when he agreed to leave his beloved but ever so foolish wife behind and to return to America alone, he admitted not only that he had been defeated and that his way of life had been rejected, but also that the two worlds had nothing in common and that it was far more than the

Atlantic Ocean that separated the Middle West from the Riviera.

In Booth Tarkington's *The Plutocrat*, however, the cleavage was mended at least in part, for though the American capitalist Earl Tinker, on a Mediterranean cruise, felt uncomfortable and contemptuous amidst the smoothness and the shallowness of European socialites and aestheticizing American expatriates, and had no real appreciation even of the culture of Greece, his outlook changed completely when, in Italy and in the sand-covered ruins of North Africa, he discovered the lasting traces of the Roman Empire of bygone centuries. He worshipped and fully understood the greatness of ancient Rome, for Romans, like Americans, were essentially men of deeds and not of words, engineers and statesmen rather than philosophers and artists, empire-builders who built grandiosely and lastingly, for the greatest comfort of the greatest number of people – highways, aqueducts, cities, canals and theatres – and who were unrelenting in pushing on and on the frontiers of the kind of civilization they knew. Today, our reverence for classical antiquity embraces both Greece and Rome, for though Greek culture served as the basis of the civilization of Rome also, the genius of Rome had added a political wisdom and statesmanship of its own, which is no less deserving of our admiration – and Booth Tarkington leaves us with the reassuring feeling that a similar close relationship exists also between the spiritual foundation of Europe and the material expansion and achievement of America.

Indeed we can say that the two are complementary, each one adding to the rich and complex texture of the Western World that which it is best qualified to give – and what, at times, seem to be unbridgeable contrasts and differences of emphasis will, in the eyes of posterity, flow together as facets of the same basic Western culture of the twentieth century. The scope of that culture is sufficiently wide and flexible to allow for differences of approach and expression; there is ample room as well as ample need, not only for the supreme art of Michelangelo and the wisdom of Goethe, but also for the constructive statesmanship of Thomas Jefferson and the ingenious technical inventions of Thomas Alva Edison. The two are inseparable; they are the foundation of our modern way of life.

ABRIDGED INDEX

Oregon, U of 9
Orsini, G. N. 8, 49

Parkman, F. 57
Pellegrini, C. 46
Poe, E. A. 142, 143
Prescott, W. H. 142
Price, L. M. 4, 6

Racine, J. 103ff
Remak, H. H. H. 37
Revue de Littérature comparée 10, 37
Rousseau, J.-J. 65

Schiller, F. 121, 123
Schlegel, A. W. 74
Seidlin, O. 49
Shackleton, R. 46
Sismondi, J. C. L. 75
Smit, W. A. P. 46
Sophocles 97-101

Staël, Mme de 38, 73, 74, 75
Strich, F. 22, 88, 108
Switzerland 38, 58, 61ff

Tarkington, B. 150
Thompson, S. 4, 5

van Tieghem, P. 26, 38, 40, 47, 61
Voisine, J. 46

Wellek, R. 5, 7, 9, 26, 37, 39, 46, 49
Whitman, W. 144
Wisconsin, U of 8, 25
World Literature 15, 25ff

Yale U 7, 38, 44
Yearbook of Comparative and General Literature
    12, 13, 26, 49

Zürich 67, 68, 69, 72, 76